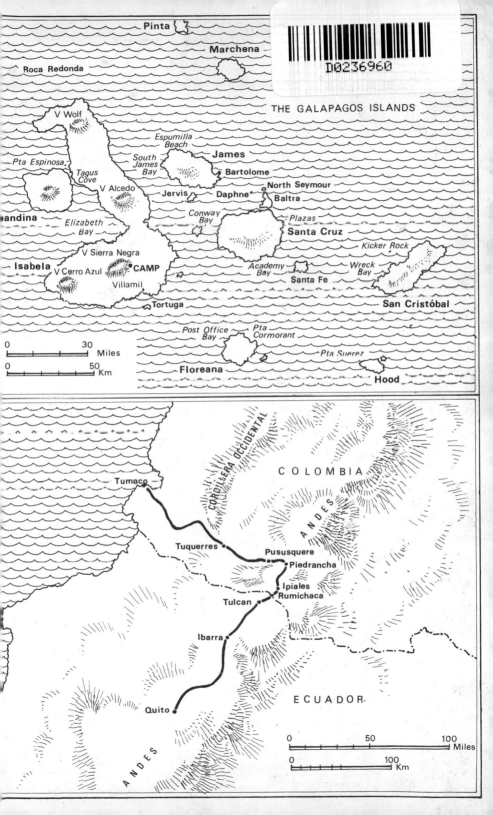

THE GALAPAGOS ISLANDS

Pinta

Marchena

Roca Redonda

V Wolf

Espumilla
Beach

Pta Espinosa

South
James
Bay

James

Bartolome

...andina

Tagus
Cove

V Alcedo

Jervis

Daphne

North Seymour

Baltra

Conway
Bay

Plazas

Elizabeth
Bay

Santa Cruz

Kicker Rock

V Sierra Negra

Isabela

V Cerro Azul

CAMP

Academy
Bay

Santa Fe

Wreck
Bay

Villamil

San Cristóbal

Tortuga

Post Office
Bay

Pta
Cormorant

Pta Suerez

0   30 Miles

0   50 Km

Floreana

Hood

CORDILLERA OCCIDENTAL

COLOMBIA

Tumaco

ANDES

Tuquerres

Pususquere

Piedrancha

Ipiales

Rumichaca

Tulcan

Ibarra

ECUADOR

ANDES

Quito

0   50   100 Miles

0   100 Km

The Voyager

Also by the same author:

THE ISLANDER

The Voyager

**The Further Adventures of the Man who Wanted
to be Robinson Crusoe**

Gerald Kingsland

NEW ENGLISH LIBRARY

First published in Great Britain in 1987 by
New English Library, Mill Road, Dunton Green, Sevenoaks, Kent.
Editorial office: 47 Bedford Square, London WC1B 3DP.

Typeset by Rowland Phototypesetting Limited,
Bury St Edmunds, Suffolk.
Printed in Great Britain by St Edmundsbury Press Limited,
Bury St Edmunds, Suffolk.

British Library Cataloguing in Publication Data

Kingsland, Gerald
   The voyager: the further adventures of
   the man who wanted to be Robinson
   Crusoe.
   1. Islands of the Pacific – Description and travel
   I. Title
   919'.04   DU23.5

ISBN 0-450-40656-3

For Yeannie, Rory and Redmond

The Voyager

1

The *alcalde* – head of the community – rather resembled Humphrey Bogart. As though to prove it, he flattened his top lip against his teeth, Bogart fashion.

'You are very lucky,' he told us in Spanish. 'Until only a few weeks ago, bands of communists were always terrorising this district, shooting and robbing people as they pleased. You are white and you would have been prime targets.' He perched himself on the edge of the chief of police's desk and added, with self-satisfaction: 'But we have exterminated them.'

Behind the desk, nodding a massive head on a bull neck in smug confirmation, the chief of police looked as though he could easily exterminate anything or anybody. His olive-green uniform bulged in huge corrugations across his enormous body, and a .45 revolver in leather holster hung from a cinch-like belt round his expansive middle to halfway down the chair's legs. Definitely not a man to be trifled with, I thought.

The *alcalde* took a twenty-pack of Redskin cigarettes from his sports jacket pocket and continued, with another Bogart grimace: 'Nonetheless, I would strongly advise that you four people always keep close together; don't venture out alone, especially at night. You are the first foreigners ever to live in Pususquere. That is quite something. The village people are frightened of you; they think that perhaps you, too, are terrorists, and they would have no hesitation in killing you if they thought you were a threat to them. And there would be nothing I could do.'

In a gesture of apology for his words, the *alcalde* proffered his cigarettes. Only I and the chief accepted. Redmond, my nineteen-year-old son, and Yeannic were non-smokers. Yeannie was the young Chilean woman with

9

whom I had fallen in love – and she with me – on the
Galapagos Islands four months previously. My other son,
Rory, aged twenty, had stayed behind to protect
our belongings in the wooden shack we were renting for
about £3.50 a month in Pususquere, seven kilometres
away.

From the other side of the chief's roomy office, with its
array of diplomas, portrait of Bolivar, *El Libertador*, and
glass-fronted cabinet containing rifles with a chain through
the trigger guards, Redmond regarded me with a look
which could only mean: 'Thanks, Dad, for bringing us to
a God-forsaken place like this.' On Yeannie's face was
simply love and an expression of *que será*.

I turned to the *alcalde*. 'But surely,' I protested, 'the
people will know, after our visit to the chief's office here
in Piedrancha, that we are harmless and not terrorists.'

'Yes,' replied the *alcalde*, lighting my cigarette with a
silver lighter and going into the Bogart act with his top
lip, 'the intelligent ones will know that.' He put emphasis
on the word 'intelligent'. 'But there are very few intelligent
people in Pususquere. The ignorant ones are the majority
and they are the ones you must watch out for. It will be
hard to convince them that you are not terrorists. Why
else are you here? Tourists do not come to Piedrancha,
and certainly not to Pususquere. Your presence here is
difficult to explain even to the intelligent.'

I fully appreciated what he said. It was difficult enough
to explain to anybody, intelligent or otherwise, exactly
why we were in this remote and dangerous part of Nariño
Province in the southern Colombian Andes with less than
£100 between us and no return air tickets. How could I
tell someone who did not speak my native tongue, especially an *alcalde* or chief of police, that it was partly
because of my pig-headedness in not heeding a country's
rules and regulations, partly because of a stupid mistake
on my part, and partly because of my trying to realise a
long-standing dream which, once again, had not material-
ised?

'As I told the chief of police before you arrived,' I said,

simply and succinctly, 'all I want to do is build a boat and get back to England.'

The *alcalde* took his cigarette from his mouth. 'But you are 170 kilometres from our nearest port!' he exclaimed.

Yeannie, born in a Spanish-speaking country, decided to venture the same explanation as she had given to the impassive chief of police during his intensive questioning of us earlier. Afterwards the chief, not quite sure of the situation, had summoned the *alcalde* to his office.

'My husband (she always referred to me as such) is an author. He writes about his adventures. He thinks it would be a beautiful story if he built a boat in this little-known part of Colombia, transported it to the sea, and sailed it to England.'

It hadn't started off that way – quite a lot had happened before that. But what she said sufficed. The *alcalde* regarded me with new-found respect at the mention of the word author. He gave two Bogart grimaces in quick succession.

'An author, eh?' he said. 'Fantastic! I appreciate the arts very much. Little opportunity to study them here. But in our capital cities we have plenty. Also, the world has always needed adventurers and explorers.'

He wanted to know what I had written so far. Yeannie told him that a book of mine had just been published about my attempts to be a second Robinson Crusoe with three different young women on three different uninhabited islands. She seemed to dwell on the 'young women' aspect, much to the amusement of the *alcalde* and the chief. The three of them were engaged in exchanges of Spanish far too rapid for me to grasp more than the gist of what was said. Judging by the laughter, I gathered it was good PR work on her part.

'Splendid. Splendid,' said the *alcalde*, eventually. 'Of course you are welcome to build your boat in Pususquere, provided you remember what I have said. Always proceed with suavity, be tranquil, have respect for the villagers and their ways, and always keep together.' Ignoring the ashtray on the chief's desk, he flicked his cigarette ash on to the

11

floor. Surreptitiously, I followed suit. The floor was of bare boards and needed sweeping anyway.

There was silence while the *alcalde* manipulated his top lip. Then a thought seemed to strike him. 'Ah!' he said. 'What about transport when you have built your boat? Incidentally, I take it you have sufficient experience and qualifications to build a boat?' My nod was only a half lie. The *alcalde* accepted my nod and went on with his train of thought: 'The road through the jungle to the coast is very, very bad – even worse than here. The journey takes a minimum of twelve hours. It will cost you a lot of money to take a boat through there.'

'I was given to understand,' I said, and this was no lie, 'that wood was so cheap here that it would more than compensate for transportation costs. Also, the Guerrero family would help me to get a cheap lorry.'

'Perhaps. Perhaps,' said the *alcalde*, with something akin to disbelief. 'But wood is much cheaper in the port of Tumaco. It grows there and is brought to here.'

'I didn't know that,' I said.

'Also, you would constantly have to guard your materials in Pususquere in case they were stolen. I think it would be less expensive for you if you went to Tumaco. No transport problems; and, possibly, Tumaco would be safer for you. Americans live there and the people are used to tourists. Perhaps you could persuade an American to assist you and allow you to build your boat on his premises.'

'What is Tumaco like?' asked Yeannie.

'A big port – many industries – very hot. But I must warn you of one thing: 80 per cent of the population are negroes. There are many problems and many murders.'

'Are there major banks in Tumaco?' Yeannie asked. 'We have few pesos and need to change English pounds.' Had she said how many pounds we would probably have been deported immediately as vagrants!

'Oh, yes,' said the *alcalde*, 'there are many banks in Tumaco.' He paused for the Bogart act. 'One thing I would very much like to know,' he continued, on a completely

12

different topic, sending twin streams of smoke down his nostrils, 'is what brought you to this little-known part of Colombia in the first place.'

Giving me a 'here goes for nothing' look, Yeannie launched into an explanation. I knew that some of it would be a lie.

'The original adventure,' said Yeannie, 'began last November – three months ago – when we went to the Galapagos Islands.'

'That is where they have the giant tortoises and prehistoric iguanas?' interrupted the *alcalde*.

'Yes,' said Yeannie, and she launched into a romantic-eyed account of those equatorial islands that are also known as the 'Enchanted Isles'.

'Ah, a paradise,' murmured the *alcalde* when she had finished – and even the chief's black eyes had a faraway look.

'Yes,' replied Yeannie, doubtfully. 'In a way, that is . . .'

'How do you mean?' prompted the *alcalde*, flicking more ash on to the floor.

Yeannie gave me a short look, then went on to explain why the islands had not been suitable for our twin projects of living the existentialist dream and building a boat to sail to England. Of course, she did not divulge the real reason why we had been forced to leave.

'So what did you do?' asked the *alcalde*.

'Returned to the mainland – to Ecuador's capital, Quito, where I have several friends – and looked for another place to build our boat. By now, for Gerald and his two sons, the boat had become the main project. We were investigating the possibility of the Amazon and an island off the southern coast of Ecuador when we met Lola Guerrero. She was working in Quito. When she heard that we wanted to build a boat and sail it to England, she said her parents' farm in Pususquere would be the ideal place – and she brought us here.'

'Well, I wish you very much luck, whatever you decide to do,' said the *alcalde*, easing himself off the desk as

13

signal that the interview was over. He dropped what was left of his cigarette on to the floor and put his foot on it. Offering his hand to me first, he looked me straight in the eye, flattening his top lip against his teeth as he did so. I thought his handshake was firm and sincere. 'One further warning,' he said. 'If you do go to Tumaco, keep well away from the negroes.'

The chief also shook our hands and gave us back our passports. We stepped out into the hot, dusty, unpaved street. Everything shimmered in the one o'clock sun. Flicking my cigarette end to join other debris, I said to Redmond: 'Well, my old darling, I take it you got the drift of what was said?'

'If you mean do I know that we are in the shit – yes,' he said.

'Correct,' I replied. 'We are what is termed between Scylla and Charybdis – or, more simply, for your bovine brain, between a devil of a situation and, literally, the deep blue sea.'

'If only we could go back to Ecuador,' he groaned. 'At least it's civilised there.'

'We can't,' I said. 'And that's that. You know Yeannie won't be allowed back there. We've got to go on. We can't abandon her.'

'Why not?' asked Redmond.

'Don't be a twit,' I said. Yeannie apprehensively linked her arm through mine. The boys and I had had this conversation before. It was because of her that we had to leave the Galapagos. She had been in Ecuador for much longer than the permitted period stamped in her passport and no way would the authorities grant her a visa. When we had arrived at Rumichaca – the Ecuadorian–Colombian frontier town – I'd had to pay her fine for being illegal. The fine had been stamped into her passport, which made her *persona non grata* in Ecuador. It was only because Lola was with us and did a lot of talking that the Colombian authorities allowed her through on a 90-day visa, the same as us.

Not only had all this rankled with Rory and Redmond

but there was another bone of contention where Yeannie was concerned. The boys wouldn't believe that Yeannie was in love with me. Their reasoning was than an attractive woman of twenty-four would only latch on to a fifty-four-year-old man for a joy-ride to the Galapagos and to get her out of an illegal situation.

It was a difficult position for me at times. There was much love between the boys and me, and I knew I was in love with Yeannie. I had no reason to doubt her. We'd met in Chile four years previously when she was only twenty and at university in Temuco. I also knew her parents and her brothers. There had been great attraction between Yeannie and me even then, but I had walked away from it. Twenty years was much too young an age . . .

Redmond turned his aggression to Lola – although that young woman had returned to Quito.

'There are two things I'd like to do right now, Dad,' he growled. 'Wring Lola's neck and get on the "big white bird that flies" back to England.'

'We don't have any money,' I reminded him. 'Besides, if we went back to England now I wouldn't have a story to write. So far as I can see, there's no book in our Galapagos experiences. It's all been said before. We'll just have to weather it and hope that at the end I'll have a book – and get back all the bloody money I've spent on fares, hotels and provisions.'

'Well, what are we going to do?' demanded Redmond. 'Stay in this shit-hole or go to another one on the coast?'

'Let's wait until we get back to Rory. Discuss it fully and put down all the pros and cons. In the meantime, we deserve a beer – and we'll find out what time the bus goes. Yeannie did pretty well in the chief's office, don't you think?'

Redmond just grunted. I kissed Yeannie's cheek. 'You were marvellous,' I told her.

As we expected, people stared fixedly at us as we walked along the street. We had experienced this every day during the week we had been in the district, and it was something we could not adjust to.

15

'Why do they look at us with such hostile eyes?' Yeannie asked, nervously.

'I don't think it's so much hostility as plain curiosity,' I told her, comfortingly.

'Well, it gives me the shits,' declared Redmond.

Now and again we caught the disdainful whisper: 'Gringos.' Most of the buildings were ramshackle, their timbers blackened, cracked and warped by the extremes of cold and heat. Everywhere was poverty.

We made for a paint-faded wooden sign which barely announced 'Café-Restaurant'. Chickens squawked and ran out through the back door as we entered. Two women behind a lop-sided counter regarded us as though we had crawled out from under a rock. Redmond and I nudged Yeannie forward as spokeswoman. 'Three beers, please,' she said.

The table we sat at was scarred and scored, and beneath it was hen-shit. But the beer was bottled. We ignored the wet glasses that were also plonked on the table. The two women watched our every swig.

'What time is the next bus to Pususquere?' Yeannie asked, pleasantly.

'Six o'clock,' came the laconic reply.

'Jesus Christ!' said Redmond.

'Of course,' said Yeannie, in dismay. 'It's Sunday! Let's walk back! It's downhill all the way through the valley, and it's better than staying here all afternoon and being stared at.'

Redmond and I agreed. It would only take us two hours. We would be back by mid-afternoon. If we waited until six, Rory would start fretting. Probably think we had been thrown into jail. It was only that morning that the local policeman and two other men – all armed – had banged on our door, demanding to see our passports. They had searched our belongings and found three lethal sheath knives and a powerful air rifle. Yeannie had quickly ex- plained about the Galapagos adventure.

The policeman had said that was all right as far as he was concerned, but it was his chief in Piedrancha who

16

would have to decide. We must present our passports to him immediately. After further discussion with Yeannie he consented to Rory's staying behind to watch our possessions.

It was on the walk back to Pususquere that I learned that Redmond did have some affection for Yeannie. We passed by a nursery for coffee plants. 'Hey!' I said to Yeannie, 'You forgot to tell the *alcalde* that we had a coffee plantation on Isabela.'

'Oh, I'd love a Colombian coffee plant,' she said. 'I really would.'

Redmond was the only one with pesos. All my money was English. 'All right,' said Redmond, 'I'll buy you one.' And he did.

'We have got to get this plant to England,' said Yeannie, holding it lovingly in its plastic bag filled with Colombian soil. 'It will be our emblem.'

'Sentimental bitch,' said Redmond.

But I knew he didn't mean it.

2

Like Redmond, Rory is six-foot-one in height and has good shoulders to match. But the similarity ends there. Redmond has black hair. Rory's is the colour of bleached corn. Redmond's manner is easy-going, jocular except for bellicose bouts. Rory's is more taciturn – aggressive when he needs to hide emotion. I knew by his angry greeting, 'Where the hell have you been?' that he had been extremely worried about us. He had been sitting on the rotting-timbered verandah, scanning the long road for a dust cloud that would signify an approaching vehicle. He didn't move when we rounded the final bend, dragging tired legs. Seven kilometres is a long way under a hot sun. Yeannie was limping because her shoes had blistered her heels.

Rory still sat with a scowl on his face as I explained about the absence of Sunday buses. I continued, with levity: 'We have some good news and some bad news. Which do you want first?'

'Give me the bad news,' he said, but his belligerence was partly pretended. Had things been serious, he knew I wouldn't have used the joke.

'The bad news is,' I said, pausing for effect, 'there isn't any good news!'

'I suppose we are all going to be deported because of her,' grumbled Rory, with some semblance of humour.

'There *is* good news, Rory,' said Yeannie. 'Look! We have our passports.' And she took them from her leather handbag. 'And see what Redmond bought me!' Pointing to the plant Redmond was carrying.

'What's *that*?' snorted Rory.

'A Colombian coffee plant,' said Yeannie. 'We are going to take it to England. It will be our mascot on the boat.'

Another snort from Rory. Then his expression brightened. 'So we *can* build our boat?'

I nodded. 'Make some tea – there's a good boy – and we'll tell you what happened.'

'The water's been boiling for hours,' he said.

In the comparative cool of our dilapidated kitchen at the rear of the shack, after he'd heard all that the *alcalde* had said, he shook his head. 'I don't know, Dad. This place gives me the creeps. It's all right for you, you've been in a war, you've been used to this sort of life. But I haven't. I'm too young to die!'

'Aw, come on,' I said, 'no one's tried to kill you yet. It's not such a bad situation. We'll get through all right, so long as we stick together – like The Three Musketeers: all for one, and one for all.'

'And she's Dark Onion, I suppose,' said Redmond, indicating Yeannie. As a little boy, he'd never been able to pronounce 'd'Artagnan', and it had become a joke.

'Ah,' said Yeannie. *'Los Tres Mosqueteros!'* Although she had difficulty in speaking English, she could understand quite a lot of it. The conversation between her and the boys was a mixture of pidgin English and pidgin Spanish, with many invented words. (To help the reader I've standardised her speech.)

'No, you little fart,' said Redmond. 'The Three Musketeers – not *Los Tres Mosqueteros*. If you don't learn to speak English, how are you going to order us drinks in the Hop Pole Hotel in Bromyard?'

Yeannie showed her perfect, white teeth in a charming smile. 'Sree peents of Pedigree ayel, plees, and a glass of Germany wine,' she said, proudly.

'Ooo!' groaned Redmond. 'She'll never learn, Dad.'

'Yes she will. Leave her alone. I don't know how she puts up with all your insults – why she doesn't slap your face.'

'Because she's only five-foot-fuck-all,' said Redmond, patting the top of her head. 'She wouldn't dare, would you, little titchy?'

19

She made to slap him in fun. He grabbed her wrist and twisted it. As soon as she yelled, he let go.

'I think that Yeannie's a damn sight tougher than you two,' I said. 'She never complains – and she washes your clothes in cold water. I think she's a good sport.'

'You would,' said Rory. 'Besides, they wouldn't hurt her if they decided to kill us. She's South American – one of them.'

'Yeah,' said Redmond. 'They'd probably give her a good fucking and let her go.'

'Redmond!' Yeannie remonstrated, coughing out a mouthful of tea.

'Yes, Redmond,' I said, feeling my anger rise. 'That was a bit much. Now pack it up – both of you. What we have to decide is, what are we going to do?'

A dreamy look was still on Rory's face after the mention of the Hop Pole Hotel. 'Right now,' he said, 'I'd like to be back in beautiful, peaceful Herefordshire. I'd be all nice and clean.'

'And freezing cold,' I added. 'It's February, remember.'

He ignored me. 'Then I'd get on the bike and bomb down to the Hop Pole for a Sunday session. A pint of Pedigree, please, Peter! Instead, I'm sitting in this hovel, drinking this muck.'

'Well, you made it,' I said. 'I must admit though, that a pint of Pedigree would go down exceedingly well.'

'Ahh!' breathed Redmond.

'And a glass of Germany wine for me,' chipped in Yeannie.

'Yes,' I said, smiling. 'A big glass of German wine for you.'

We sat in silence with our individual thoughts. 'Come on!' I said. 'Let's have some points of view.'

'One thing's for sure,' ventured Rory, 'we don't like this place. It's freezing cold at night and we're in a house – if you can call it that – without beds and furniture. Also, everybody stares at us when we go out, and that gets on my nerves.'

'And I don't like living with people who eat their pet

20

guinea pigs,' said Redmond. 'It's bloody revolting. I'll never be able to look at another guinea pig.'

That first evening had been a positive shock to our systems. We all held a vivid memory of our arrival at the house of Mercedes Guerrero, mother of Lola, after a nineteen-hour journey from Quito in two buses and, finally, in a dust-filled jeep-taxi. We were very tired and hungry. The irony of it was that we had passed through some really beautiful countryside before we got to Pususquere. Even the valley road from Piedrancha was lovely. Then we hit Pususquere. It was a dump – the ugliest part of the valley.

'I was very excited on the last part of the journey,' said Yeannie. 'I was looking for Lola's beautiful farm. I think she was a little crazy with her description.'

'Crazy?' echoed Rory. 'She was bloody demented.'

'What is demented?' asked Yeannie.

'More crazy than crazy,' I said. 'But I don't think Lola was crazy – I think she was quite clever. She got a free return trip to visit her family because I paid for it!'

Mercedes and her husband had parted company. He lived as a quite contented bachelor at the other end of the village. 'At least, he's got sense,' commented Redmond. 'Fancy having to spend your life with her and in that house!'

Like all the houses in Pususquere, Mercedes' house was of black wood, built on stilts. None of the houses had chimneys, yet all had fires inside. The smoke just filtered out through the eaves – but not before it had coated the underside of the roof with soot! The rising vapour from cooking fat and the steam from cauldrons added a wet, shiny coat to the black. With the flickering lights of the flames and candles – there were no windows – illuminating the myriad of spiders' webs on the beams and rafters, it was all rather awesome.

'Even Mercedes toned in with the background and ceiling,' said Rory. She did, too. She was dressed all in black. With a jaw like Mr Punch, she looked like an old witch as she stirred what was in the black pot. Running around the

21

anything but clean floor were a dozen or so guinea pigs, eating sugar cane and shitting it out almost as soon as they took it in.

Mercedes had told us to sit down round a small, black table. Yeannie instinctively rubbed it with the palm of her hand. We did the same. It felt greasy. Mercedes doled out the soup. Yeannie sniffed it. 'Very rich,' she complimented the old woman. In the soup were tiny pieces of whitish meat. We all tasted it. Without doubt, it was very good. When we'd finished eating, Yeannie began cooing and calling to the guinea pigs.

'You like them?' asked Mercedes.

'Oh, yes,' said Yeannie. 'They're lovely.'

'One was in the soup,' said the old girl, cackling.

Horror and revulsion had spread over all our faces.

'I feel ill,' moaned Rory.

'Me, too,' wailed Yeannie.

'Sit still,' I said. 'Wait for a while to be polite, then we'll all go outside for a good spew! How's my little darling Redmond feeling?' And I began laughing at the absurdity of it all.

'Piss off!' Redmond hissed at me.

The old girl laughed, too. 'I will roast you two nice ones now,' she said. Her gnarled hands grabbed the two guinea pigs nearest to her. One was brown and white, the other a yellowy-orange. She held them tight as they squealed and kicked, then she banged the backs of their necks hard on the iron surround of the fireplace. They were quite dead when she popped them into near-boiling water. With the help of a kitchen knife as scraper, the fur came off quite easily. The two guinea pigs looked like deathly-white, premature embryos. With the point of the knife, Mercedes made a tiny hole in the first one's belly. She squeezed, and the intestines and bowels came worming out like toothpaste from the tube.

'I'm getting out of here,' said Rory, rising.

I quickly told Yeannie to apologise to the old girl – that we were very tired and we were going to take some fresh air before going to bed.

22

'No problem,' Mercedes answered her. 'My house is your house.'

The sky was full of stars. We took many, many gulps of the already very cold air. 'Some experience, eh?' I commented. No one answered. 'I think,' I went on, reflectively, 'that it is a question of the senses being affected by a touch of the macabre. If everything had been clean – if the guinea pigs hadn't been running about in their own shit – if we had shot one in the cleanliness of a field – it wouldn't have been half as bad. But to keep them in the house as pets, with the kids playing with them one minute and the old girl killing them the next . . .'

'Shut up, Dad,' said Redmond, 'I want to forget.'

'The house is a bloody pig-sty!' Rory had spat out the words. 'And we've got to sleep in it.'

'Quite right, my son,' I said. 'It *is* a pig-sty. A guinea pig-sty!'

'Ha, ha,' said Redmond, sarcastically. 'Very, very funny.'

Lola hadn't sat with us at the table but had squatted on the floor next to the fire with the rest of the family, made up, from what I could gather, of her bastards, her brother's bastards and others of dubious parentage. She joined us outside. Yeannie told her that we all felt sick and revolted about the guinea pigs. She laughed. 'I have something to cure your stomachs,' she said. 'Come back to the house.'

And that was how we were introduced to '*anisado*', the local firewater which, I'm sure, would melt your fingernails!

'Wow! It's lethal, Dad,' Rory had exclaimed, after his first sip. And it had certainly made sleeping wrapped in our own blankets on the dirty bedroom floor in Mercedes' house much more tolerable.

For the whole week we had been in the village, any topic of conversation seemed to veer back to that first night and the guinea pigs, as it was doing now.

Getting back to the present, I said: 'If the man at the shop up the road can't change our English money when he goes to Ipiales tomorrow, we'll have to go to Tumaco.

I think everything hinges on that,' Ipiales was the Colombian town nearest to the Ecuadorian border. Every Monday, the man in the local shop made the seven-hour return journey to buy his wares. Yeannie had been instrumental in finding out that information.

'How much are you going to give him, Dad?' asked Redmond.

'£30,' I said. 'How many pesos have you got left?'

He took the notes from his pocket and counted them. '4,700, plus rubbishy money.'

'Good,' I said. 'Now then, if we do decide to go to Tumaco, I think we should go a week tomorrow – Monday. I don't want to arrive in a strange place at a weekend when banks are shut – nor in the middle of the week. We want as many working days as possible before a weekend to have a good look round. Saturdays and Sundays are always hopeless for finding out things – everything stops for the weekend.'

'Dad,' said Rory, 'I vote that we go to Tumaco in any case. We need to be in touch with England. We need more money. We've costed out the boat: £75, which is incredible for a 25-foot sailer – but we've got to live as well. There are no telephones here, and God knows how long a letter would take. If it had been as Lola said – that we wouldn't have to worry about food because we'd work on her mother's farm for our keep – that would have been all right. But I hate it here, living like this. The only true thing she said about this place was the cheapness of wood. But probably even that has wood-worm! And she didn't mention it was cheaper in Tumaco.'

I looked at Redmond for his opinion.

'I want to be warm at night,' he said, 'and feel safe like we were on the Galapagos. It's always cleaner by the sea – we could even sleep on the beach, if necessary. All these people carry machetes and most of them look at you as though they could cheerfully cut your throat. Even the son of the man we rent this shack from is in jail for murder. We are not wanted here – that's for sure. I say we go to Tumaco.'

24

'What about you, Yeannie?' I asked.

'I don't like the thought of Tumaco, as the *alcalde* described it, with its problems and murders,' she said, 'but I don't like it here. I am very frightened at night. We have to put wood across the doors for safety and we sleep with knives under our pillows. It is not a good life. We have no toilet – we have to shit outside in the sugar-cane plantation, and those little flies bite my arse. The other morning, one bit the end of Gerald's cock!' Much laughter at that. 'I think we should go to Tumaco. I think, too, that the *alcalde* prefers that we do.'

'Well, that's it, then,' I said. 'We'll go a week tomorrow. I think it's the best decision all round. As the *alcalde* said, no worries about transportation and there are banks so that we can get more money. Then we can afford to build a 38-footer, as I really want to do. In fact, we'll start designing it right now. We'll make the hull a deep-vee.'

'Does that mean we scrap the present design?' Rory asked, mournfully.

'Yep. We have to start all over again if you want a really nice boat.'

'I hate working out the angles of all the ribs,' he complained. 'Why doesn't Redmond ever help?'

'Because I'm the carpenter,' said Redmond. 'You two are the designers.'

'Besides,' I said to Rory, 'it keeps your brain working.'

Yeannie and Redmond elected to cook an early dinner: tinned sardines, chips and fried onions. 'And I think it's time for a nice glass of *anisado*,' I announced. 'Solely for inspiration!'

'Piss head!' said Redmond. 'How can you drink that stuff on an empty stomach?'

'It needs great practice,' I retorted. 'It's the only thing that keeps me sane; and at the equivalent of 70 pence a litre we can afford it.' I took the bottle out from under something that could be described as shelves, where it was cool in the daytime. There was little more than a glassful left. 'Rory! You bugger!' I said.

'I had a little drop to keep my morale up while you were out,' he admitted, grinning.

'When we go to the shop after dinner to give the man the money,' I said, 'we'll have to call on Tia Maria.'

Tia Maria – Lola's Aunt Mary, not the liqueur – was an illicit *anisado* maker. Or rather, her daughter was. That first time we had entered her dwelling had proved to be another gruesome experience of how the people of Pususquere lived.

Lola had told us about her aunt. 'But don't pay more than 100 pesos for a litre,' she'd said. 'That's the correct price.'

On our third night in the village just as it was getting dark, carrying an empty bottle we had trooped across the dirt road from Mercedes' house to the one opposite. At Yeannie's rap on the door, a shrill voice had commanded us to enter. Inside, the one-room, rickety building was like a smoke-filled cave. Shiny black ceiling and walls, adorned with enormous cobwebs, and the inevitable guinea pigs scurrying hither and thither over the earthen floor. Dirt-caked and cobweb-entwined bottles were everywhere. In the centre, attending to an illicit still over the wood fire – which gave the only light – was Tia Maria's elderly, hump-backed daughter.

'How beautiful!' said Yeannie, to our amazement. Possibly, fright induced the inane remark.

Then, from behind us came a croaked '*Buenas noches*'. We turned, and recoiled with the same shock as if we had seen a ghost. Trying to sit up in bed – and failing – a long, bony arm reaching out to us, was a ghostly apparition called Tia Maria. The scene was like something out of Edgar Allen Poe. Her toothless head resembled a skull with the fire's flames highlighting the white cheekbones and making black hollows of her eyes.

'*Buenas noches*,' we replied, hoarsely.

Yeannie plucked up the courage to approach the bed, which was against the wall behind the door. I went with her and we found that Tia Maria was still with the living after all. In fact, she was quite cognisant. She apologised for not getting up, but she wasn't feeling too good. It was her age, she explained. She was 105!

Thankfully, the daughter quickly filled our bottle and Redmond paid the 100 pesos. We couldn't wait to get outside. We felt sick with the stench and heat, and our eyes were stinging from the smoke.

Outside, Redmond said: 'You know why the old bitch's lived so long? She's pickled in smoke and *anisado*.'

'And guinea pigs,' added Rory.

The scene had been the same the several times we had called there. The *anisado* was only ready just before dusk, for in the daytime the daughter worked in the cane field. It was from the first, crude extraction of the brown sugar – *panela* – that the *anisado* was distilled and the aniseed added. This gave it a taste similar to an imagined mixture of liquorice and battery acid! I found it best always not to allow the clear, white liquid to stay in the mouth but to knock it straight back, allowing the stomach to bear the brunt of the fiery pain the initial gulp always produced. I was reminded of a doctor friend's description once of a new tranquilliser. 'This potent little pill,' he said, 'makes the inside of a nut-house seem like a palace to the inmates.' And, certainly, the *anisado* made Pususquere seem a much nicer place to me.

3

It wasn't until our third day in Pususquere – and only four hours before Lola left to go back to Quito – that we found a house to stay in. For two days we had been forced to nag her to find us a place. 'You brought us here,' I told her, sternly, 'with the promise of many things, including one of your aunts' houses. I accept the fact that you didn't know the house had been rented out, but we *must* have somewhere to live. You know Yeannie can't return to Ecuador.'

So for two days she and Yeannie had asked owners of the few empty houses in the village for permission for us to rent one. But always there had been excuses why we couldn't. Then, luckily for us, a friend of the Guerreros came down from his mountain home, where he had a sugar mill, and said we could have his old house. He didn't much care to live in the village after his son's conviction for murder. With relief, we immediately gave him 500 pesos for a month's rent in advance.

The house was about a kilometre from the shop and a little further from the centre of the village where Mercedes and Tia Maria lived. We had nine pieces of luggage, including two large boxes of provisions, cutlery, china and cooking utensils. The thought of lugging it all that way was depressing. Lola's brother said that, if we waited until the next day, he would get a horse for us.

At ten o'clock the next morning, with our belongings piled high on a hod-like contraption on the horse's back, and me leading the horse by a rope halter, we set off, rather self-consciously, down the road through an avenue of a thousand eyes, or, as Redmond crudely put it: 'Down the street of a thousand arseholes!'

The house was T-shaped with three fair-sized rooms

forming the top of the T and the kitchen making the stem. The front verandah was only a few feet from the road and was thick with dust from passing traffic. The ground sloped down from the road, the house being kept vertical by progressively longer stilts. Inside, everything was filthy.

The back of the house where the kitchen was situated was some six feet off the ground. An old ladder was the means of getting in and out at the rear. We went down it to inspect the soundness of the stilts. That was when we heard 'the voice'. None of us, including Yeannie, could understand what it said; and we couldn't fathom out where it came from. Another house was at the side of ours, only a few yards away and without a dividing fence. We scanned it but still could see no one. And still the voice continued, unintelligibly.

Suddenly, Yeannie said: 'Look at the crack in the boards on the left-hand side of the house – about three feet up!'

We looked, and could just make out a pair of eyes. '*Buenos dias!*' Yeannie called out to the eyes. 'How are you?' The eyes disappeared. Then the voice came from the front corner of the house and round it emerged a dwarf of a woman who looked as if she had been dragged through the proverbial hedge – and a muddy ditch – backwards. Her bare feet and hairy legs were begrimed, and her hair looked a haven for lice. She walked towards us, scratching various parts of her thin body vigorously through a tattered, faded dress.

'Here comes your new girlfriend, Rory,' said Redmond. 'What a beauty!' We were suppressing laughs when the voice spoke again. Rory instantly gave her the soubriquet 'Megaphone' for she sounded just like those door phones that splutter out something indecipherable when you ring the bell. The boys and I never did understand anything she said.

Yeannie managed to decipher her near-ultrasonic dialect. 'Megaphone' was welcoming us as neighbours and saying if there was anything she could do to help, to let her know. Yeannie asked her for a broom and bucket, and she promptly fetched them.

29

While Rory returned the horse, the three of us got busy, sweeping and scrubbing. By nightfall, the house was clean – a little damp from the number of buckets of water we used, but clean. Yeannie always maintained it was the cleanest in the village. Rory and Redmond put the back door on its hinges and repaired the door which separated the kitchen from the rest of the house to stop the smoke blackening all the rooms. Yeannie and I put the kitchen fire back in order – a wooden box filled with sand and standing on four legs, the standard design.

We took the biggest room as our bedroom, Rory's was the middle one, and Redmond's was on the other side. We used clothes as mattresses on the bare boards, put our sheets and Ecuadorian blankets on top, and stuffed woollens into pillow cases. We felt as snug as bugs when we got into bed at nights, with the sun's warmth still in the timbers, but we always awoke, cold and wretched, long before sun-up, to the raucous crow of Megaphone's cockerel, which roosted with several hens in the guayaba tree just outside our back door.

'One morning, I'm going to shoot that bastard,' Rory always promised himself.

But it was Redmond who slept with the air rifle for several nights because a big black rat had visited him as he lay reading by candlelight. One night, just as I was dozing off, I heard the rifle spit and a triumphal: 'Got you – you sod!' We all got up to look, and, sure enough, there was the rat, with a neat hole through its head – and a .22 calibre hole through the bedroom wall. Redmond had always been a good shot, and he had put paid to many a rat on the Galapagos.

Every day, Megaphone knocked on our door, wanting to know if we cared to buy firewood, milk, eggs or sugar. As her prices were a bit lower than the shop's, and we knew she could do with the money, we dealt with her. We also felt extremely sorry for her. On one or two nights her husband, a surly-looking devil, came home in a terrible mood from whatever work he did. We would hear his shouts of anger and Megaphone's wailing. Then would

come the sound of thwacks and things being smashed, and
Megaphone and the kids would start screaming. When this
happened it seemed that no sooner had we got to sleep
than the bloody cockerel began crowing!

There was one other old woman in the village that we
had great pity for. Her house was little more than the size
of a large dog kennel, yet, through the open door, it always
looked clean and tidy with many wild plants in a miscellany
of rusty tins and plastic and wooden containers. In the
mornings, she always sat hunched on the ground, just to
one side of the door, to allow the sun to warm her old
bones and to watch the passers-by. To me it always seemed
that the two things missing were a collar and a chain. It
wasn't until the Tuesday morning, when we were on our
way to the shop to see about our money, that Yeannie
had a real conversation with her – and we discovered that
some people liked our presence in the village. After her
usual happy greeting, the old woman called Yeannie over.

'I want you to know,' she said, 'that for me and my two
neighbours it is a great pleasure to see you beautiful and
colourful people walking by. Your clothes are always so
clean, and you are always polite and happy. We hope that
you will stay for a long time in Pususquere.'

Yeannie thanked her, and the old woman added, sadly:
'All my family are gone. I am alone, but my neighbours
help me. My life is now my plants – which I love – and
watching people, especially you four, passing by. Please
stop and talk to me whenever you can.' Yeannie promised
her that she would.

'I suppose,' I said, as we continued up the road, returning the numerous *buenos dias*, 'that with our height, my
red hair and Rory's yellow hair, we do look somewhat
different. Even Yeannie looks European with her hair
streaked.'

'Different?' echoed Rory. 'We look downright conspicu-
ous. Like a sixpence on a sweep's arse! Your expression,
Dad, not mine.'

'Yeah,' said Redmond. 'I reckon we'd make bloody
good targets!'

31

'Strange how people here, especially the children, want to say hello to us,' remarked Yeannie.

'Perhaps we look so peculiar to them,' I said, 'that they need to test us to see if we can talk. But it's tiring, though, when we meet a file of kids.'

'I just keep saying *buenos dias* or whatever, like a machine-gun, until the last one's passed,' said Redmond.

On our arrival at the shop, the vending part of which was only about ten feet square, the man told us that the branch banks in Ipiales were too small to change English pounds. Only head office and major branches could do so. He gave me back my £30.

'What time do the buses go to Tumaco?' Yeannie asked. 'And how much is the fare?'

'Every morning at nine o'clock,' the man replied, and added: 'Please wait a moment.' He went out and through to the living quarters.

'We'd better find out what sort of bus it is, too,' I said. South America doesn't have the same rules and regulations for motor vehicles as European countries. Most buses are rust heaps with bald tyres. Even in the civilised city of Quito, a bus is never deemed to be full until someone is sitting squashed between driver and windscreen! In rural areas, passengers swarm out on to the roof when the inside is crammed, often sharing with hobbled chickens and even a pig or two. In Pususquere we had seen buses without front mudguards and bonnets, no windows, just open framework, and steam hissing from the radiator. Because of the terrible road conditions, broken springs and axles were a regular occurrence; buses, lorries and cars often had a peculiar list. A twelve-hour journey through steaming jungle in a buckled rust bucket didn't precisely appeal.

The man's wife emerged with her usual smile. She was cleaner and more smartly dressed than the other women of the village, and to us was always charming and helpful. Cynical Rory had commented that it was because she wanted our money.

'You were asking about the fare to Tumaco?' she said.

32

'I don't know for sure, but I think it's about 500 pesos. Are you leaving us?'

'Possibly,' said Yeannie. 'We have to change our money and we would like to see what Tumaco is like. What sort of bus is it that goes there?'

'Oh, a Pullman,' was the reply. 'It goes by your house every morning. I hope you will come back to us.'

'Do you know Tumaco?'

'Yes,' said the woman. 'The beaches are beautiful – and it is very hot. But there are many negroes and many robbers.'

'Yes, I know,' said Yeannie, wistfully. 'But the *alcalde* in Piedrancha thought it better if we built our boat next to the sea.'

'I understand,' said the woman. 'When will you leave?'

'Not for another three weeks,' Yeannie lied. 'We have paid a month's rent for our house and we have enough pesos to last us till then.' I'd told her to say that. If some of the less hospitable were planning to raid us one night, they wouldn't be prompted to advance the operation.

'If you don't like Tumaco,' said the woman, 'you come back here. You have brought a certain charm to our village.'

That evening, as we sat on our verandah, watching the sun go down, the boys and Yeannie swigging beer, and me with my *anisado*, Yeannie mused: 'People *do* like us in this village.'

Rory countered her remark. 'You're just thinking of what the old woman and the woman in the shop said today. The *women* are harmless – but not the men.'

Before she could reply, I said: 'Witness, me old darlings, three classic examples approaching our establishment.'

Walking up the road towards us were three unkempt, unshaven individuals, the sort that John Wayne always shot in films. Their boots had holes; their clothes had holes. The only things reasonably clean about them were the well-honed machetes they carried.

'Most unsavoury,' commented Redmond.

33

As the three men drew level, I raised my glass. '*Buenas tardes, mis amigos,*' I said, charmingly. '*Salud!*'

One word could describe the looks they threw at me – murderous. They said nothing and carried on by.

'I don't think you should have done that,' Yeannie said, nervously.

'Why not?' I demanded. 'It's proved Rory's point. And just look at the bastards now. Still glaring back at us.'

'Dad,' said Redmond, quietly, 'I agree with Yeannie. And I don't think you should drink any more *anisado*. You've had enough for today.'

'I think maybe you're right,' I said. 'And I'm starving! Who wants to be chef?'

'I'll be fireman,' declared Rory.

'And I'll be *cocinera*,' said Yeannie. 'That is if Redmond gets the water and Gerald peels the onions!'

'Just like old times on Isabela,' I said.

On the Friday, the owner of the house arrived early in the morning, unexpectedly, and invited us to his mountain house to see how a sugar mill worked. 'I forgot to give you these,' he added, handing me two large padlocks for the front and back doors. He went outside with us and pointed out the mountain path. 'Just keep on it, right round the mountain, and you can't miss my place,' he said. 'It's the only one there. I'll be back there by mid-day, so if you start walking about ten o'clock that should be about right.'

It was quite an easy climb – though a long one – to where the path started to curve round the mountain. We stopped there and looked back over the long valley in which Pususquere lay. To our right we could see Pied-rancha. To our left, in the far distance, another village or town was visible. We all agreed that the valley was quite beautiful with its many shades of green and colourful rock formations.

We realised that it was only the drabness of the houses in Pususquere – plus the knowledge that the interiors were black and filthy – that had given us the impression of ugliness. 'You are looking,' I said, 'at the result of poverty and lack of education. That is all that's wrong with Pususquere. The people down there are just victims of circumstance, to use a cliché. They are really no different from anyone else.'

'They eat fucking guinea pigs!' stormed Redmond.

'Do you mean,' I asked, 'that they eat while copulating with guinea pigs, or that they eat copulating guinea pigs?'

'You know damn well what I mean,' he said, laughing. 'Aw, come on, Dad, you know it's revolting.'

'In select restaurants in Tokyo,' I pointed out, 'a live monkey's head is popped up through a hole in the table and secured there. Then the waiter gives it a smart bop on the head with a polished hammer and delicately cuts out a hole in the skull. The diners then dip in their spoons and eat the brains raw. That's pretty revolting, I can assure you. And once, in the Tokyo Rose Garden restaurant, when I hadn't a clue what I'd ordered, a plate of fried rice and fishes' eyeballs was placed in front of me. Whichever way I moved my plate there was always one bugger looking at me!'

'Did you eat them?' asked Rory, laughing with the others.

'Oh, yes. The simple solution to combat nausea was to turn them over and take a large gulp of saki between each one. It was quite a tasty meal, as a matter of fact. With our so-called culture, we in England are pampered. Hardly anyone would eat a cat or a dog, or even a horse . . .'

'. . . or a guinea pig!' Redmond interjected, stubbornly.

'. . . yet they are all good meat,' I continued. 'And the French eat frogs and snails. The people of Papua New Guinea eat snake, lizard and crocodile. So there you are. The English butcher's shop is really a beauty parlour for meat nowadays – the camouflage buffer between abattoir and plate. If some people saw a lovely calf's face as it was slaughtered, they'd probably never eat veal again. And most women throw away the plastic bag of offal when they buy a frozen chicken! Disgusting stuff, they say. Yet it's highly nutritional. Those people on Badu Island, where I

35

lived for five months, ate every part of an animal, bowels, intestines, the lot. And so do these people. You don't know this, but Yeannie found out that it was the guts of the guinea pig that went into our soup that night! Why are you looking green, Redmond?'

'We ate donkey on the Galapagos,' said Rory, brightly. 'And we had to kill it first! I wonder what people in England would say about that?'

'The RSPCA would probably have your guts for garters,' I said, 'and the newspapers would rave about it like they did over that chap who killed and ate his dog in the jungle when he was starving.

'I must admit, though, that if Lucy and I had had a dog on Tuin Island when we were starving, I'm pretty sure we couldn't have killed and eaten it. It's difficult to judge, though. Would you eat your dog if you were starving, Yeannie?'

'I don't know,' she said. 'I have never been starving. But I think it would depend on whether the dog was my pet. If not, possibly yes. But my pet dog, no. I think probably it would have the chance of eating me first!' And I think that summed up all our feelings on the subject.

As we continued walking, I said: 'You know, we're very scathing and critical of these people, but they are probably more content than most people in England. They may live primitively, but nobody's starving and they must be healthy or they wouldn't live so long! So what's the point of progress, medicines and washing machines, plus the eventual television set with its crap commercials telling you that if you wash your hair with a certain shampoo it will even change the wallpaper to a brighter hue? We are as bad as missionaries. When they saw people living a different and comparatively dirty sort of life, they immediately handed them a bar of soap. Missionaries have been bad buggers in this world. They've ruined many a happy society. Tahiti had a beautiful and natural attitude to sex education of the young. Then along came the missionaries and told them that God didn't like people who did that sort of thing. And no more fucks for the adolescent!'

36

'Well I don't want to live in this shit-hole,' said Rory. 'Why don't we go to Tahiti and change it back to how it was?'

Ignoring his suggestion, I went on: 'I don't want to live here, either. We've been brought up in an entirely different society. All I'm trying to say is that I don't think it's right to be hypercritical or try to change a society because the people live in houses as black as the Hole of Calcutta and appear to have a life of drudgery, when, in all likelihood, they have something the whole civilised world is constantly searching for – peace of mind.'

'Amen!' said Redmond, and he and Rory strode on ahead. Yeannie and I strolled on slowly. She agreed with me. 'Since the Conquistadores, the South American Indian has been killed, had religion forced upon him and been made to change his way of life. But in Chile – in the Ninth Region, of which Temuco is the capital – in the Andes near my father's small farm, the Indians live as they wish.'

'I remember in your mother's house in Temuco in 1980, you drew for me in my notebook a picture of the farm – the house, the barns and the fields where the different animals are kept.'

'I know,' she said. 'Why have you always kept that notebook?'

I caught hold of her. 'How many times have you asked me that? You know why. Because I've always loved you.'

She kissed me. 'I know,' she said, again. 'I love you, too. I am sorry that you didn't find your paradise on Galapagos. I am sorry I was illegal.'

'I don't mind,' I said. 'At least I've found you – and I never want to lose you.'

We carried on strolling, hand in hand. 'You know, the more I see of this world,' I said, 'the more I think it is an arsehole.'

She laughed. 'Yes. *El mundo es un culo*,' she agreed.

'In Australia,' I told her, 'I lived with the aborigines for a few weeks. Now there's a race that's been massacred, persecuted and almost annihilated. One woman, who had married an Australian white, and had won him over to their easy way of life, told me that we people of the civilised worlds were "programmed people" for commercial purposes and greed. We were conditioned to getting up at a certain time, eating breakfast, going to work, having lunch, going to work, eating dinner, a few hours of leisure, going to bed, getting up, etc. The aborigine lived and did as he wished – governed only by what he wanted to do. And that was how everyone should live – free.'

'Is that how you would like to live?' asked Yeannie. 'Is that the paradise you've always searched for on islands?'

'Yes, I think it is. I just can't stand knowing that in a so-called civilised world – no matter if I am rich, as I have been – I am still only a pawn, a puppet, controlled by invisible strings manipulated by the Corridors of Power. And I cannot stand the thought of some duke or baron paying thousands of pounds to put some woman he wants to fuck in a luxurious apartment while some poor woman with a child has to rob the gas meter to buy food. And that sort of thing is going on all the time in England.'

'Perhaps you are a communist,' suggested Yeannie.

'No. I'm sure I'm not. For with communism, too, there's always a few élite in power. And that's the same all over the civilised world.'

'Perhaps one day we will live on my father's farm,' said Yeannie. 'There you would be able to do as you liked and not be bothered by the outside world. Oh, look! Rory and Redmond are waving to us!'

As we quickened our pace to see what they wanted, Yeannie confided to me as an afterthought: 'Don't tell your sons, but we eat a lot of horse in Chile – and goats, too.'

'You heathen,' I said, laughing. 'No, of course I won't tell them.'

When we reached the boys, the other side of the mountain was in view. 'It's another world!' Yeannie exclaimed.

'That's what we thought,' said Redmond.

Not a house was in sight. The mountains and hills –

grass and bush covered – undulated for miles and miles in all directions until connecting with a blue sky. The only tell-tale sign of habitation was a wisp of smoke rising straight up from a cluster of trees level with us on the other side of the valley. The path led up to it. We went down and crossed a wide stream at the bottom by means of a narrow wooden bridge with a rope handrail on one side. We could then see that it wasn't grass as we had thought on the other slope but acres and acres of sugar cane. When we were halfway up the path, dogs began barking. A small boy came down to meet us and he escorted us past three lean, cur-like hounds to the clearing where the house stood.

Judging by the timbers and soundness of the roof, the house had been built quite recently. It stood on very high stilts. Underneath it was the mill. The smoke came from a tall, brick and cement chimney at the end of a long heat tunnel, running along the side of the mill. A large, enclosed fire was at the other end. Built into and on top of the heat tunnel were three metal cauldrons, each filled with bubbling-hot liquid sugar. The cauldron nearest the fire was the biggest and was fed by a wooden chute from a tank under the house which collected the pulped sugar liquid as the canes were crushed between two vertical iron rollers. A tap at the bottom of the tank could be turned off when the cauldron was full. Two horses turned the rollers as they walked round and round in a wide circle, pulling a radial pole which was inserted into a central drive wheel, head height from the ground. The horses' harness was simply chest bands and halters made of frayed rope.

Squatting beneath the drive wheel, a man fed in the canes, one or two at a time. The owner of our house, sweating profusely, tended the fire, stirred the first cauldron and, now and then, poured in a dark liquid. His sister, a strapping woman of about thirty-five who stirred the other cauldrons as well as cracking a whip behind the two sweating horses, showed us what the dark liquid was. The bark of a particular sapling was stripped and soaked overnight in water. This acted as a detergent and raised all impurities in the sugar to the surface in a black foam which was scooped off. When the contents of the first cauldron were considered clean, a large wooden ladle was used to put them into the two smaller ones. And there they bubbled for about half an hour until they were treacle-like in substance. This was poured into ingot-shaped moulds and allowed to cool. The result from each mould was a block of hard, browny-orange sugar called *panela*. It was all a very crude, simple – but effective – process. Cheap, too, because the squashed canes were used for the fire. It needed to be cheap, though. An ingot, weighing about half a kilo, cost only 20 pence in the shop.

The owner of our house told us: 'I don't produce enough to sell to the sugar refineries. But I make a comfortable living.' I quite liked him. Short and stocky, he seemed a quiet, honest man, and I wondered what had caused his son to commit murder. I imagined his feelings were the same as mine would be if one of my sons murdered someone.

We stayed there for about an hour, being obliged to taste the *panela* in its different and fudge-like stages. I don't have a sweet tooth and it was quite an ordeal to be polite. I had to drink water after each mouthful. But the boys and Yeannie quite enjoyed it. When we left, it felt as though sugar were coming out of the top of my head.

'Did you notice something about that house, Dad?' asked Redmond.

'Yes,' I said, wearily. 'It didn't have any guinea pigs.'

'But I bet they keep the bastards somewhere,' was the rejoinder.

4

Some days previously, at my suggestion, Rory and Redmond had begun revising the diaries they had written
during our stay on the Galapagos islands.

On Sunday morning, just before mid-day, they gave me
their new versions, with, at my request, the swear words
left out – well, most of them anyway! 'I'll sit on the
verandah and read them while I sip a pre prandial aperitif,'
I said. 'After lunch we'll have to start packing.'

Rory's account was on top of Redmond's and his opening phrase, as I settled myself in the verandah's shade,
immediately caught my eye: 'It all started when we brought
the letter from London to Dad . . .' Yes, I thought, you
are quite right, Rory, it did all start with that letter; and
I wondered if I would have acted differently had I known
the consequences.

I took several sips of *anisado*, feeling the raw alcohol
induce in me a drowsy mood of retrospection. I sat with
the boys' writings in my left hand, allowing a rapid, chrono-
logical and kaleidoscopic enactment of thought about the
events which had brought us to Pususquere, and, it would
seem, were to take us on to God knew where.

In the early Spring of 1984, after six years of travels
trying to be Robinson Crusoe, I settled, almost as a
recluse, in a caravan in a field at Rowden Paddocks,
Bromyard, Herefordshire, home of the Nosworthy family
and of Boston, the deranged ram, whose sole bent in life
was to fuck a cow.

White-haired Mary Nosworthy, mother of the household, whose family, Colebatch, dates back to 1066, explained to me about Boston: 'I bottle-fed him and he
played all day with the two pups, Moss and Mad Max,
even though they did chew his ears when they were bigger.

Boston grew up thinking he was a dog. Except for one year when he behaved as a ram (Boston had a fine son, aptly named Ivor Big'un) he's never been too sure what he is. Now he's turned his back on the sheep and dogs, and lives with the cows.'

Many a morning through my caravan window I observed Boston trying to mount a reclining cow. I would go over to him and tell him he wasn't at all nice to know, and he would regard me with his small, evil eyes. Yet, often, those eyes would hold a warmth and intelligence common in dogs, not in sheep, and, if he felt so inclined, Boston would walk with me to the gate.

Mary's husband, Frank, was in semi-retirement but in very good health except for rheumatism in his legs. Many an evening he would abandon his two sticks and take up a scythe to cut thistles and nettles in the orchard. His daily chore was to milk the cow, but if his legs were exceptionally bad I would do it for him. Peter, the black-bearded son, had taken over the farm and I would help him in the fields in repayment for my rent and food.

On Friday evenings I always repaired to the Hop Pole Hotel, run by Peter and Annie Robinson, and there I would await the arrival of Rory and Redmond, who lived with their grandparents and my eldest son, Roddick, in London. Each owned a powerful motorcycle and always my eyes would go to the clock when ten o'clock arrived and they hadn't. Then in they would come and I was at peace with the world. Saturdays they, too, helped on the farm, and Saturday night was always good in the Hop Pole. The boys and I made many friends.

Those days were truly halcyon – days for which I will always thank the Nosworthys. But, of course, there was always that certain something missing from my life – female companionship. Also, I felt in a limbo of antici- pation that surely, soon, some new adventure would start. Sensing this, Rory and Redmond made me promise that if I did go off again I would take them with me.

Then, one Friday evening in late July, as I was supping a pint in the Hop Pole, the boys arrived with the letter.

'It's from Yeannie,' said Redmond. 'She's in Ecuador.' I had often spoken to the boys about her – the girl I had first seen in a photograph in her father's cabin on Robinson Crusoe Island, where he was then head of forestry, and who I had instantly felt I had known since the Palaeolithic Age.

With excitement, I opened the envelope. She had decided to have some adventure and had been on an 18-day cruise round the Galapagos. In a Quito bookshop she had seen the very same English–Spanish phrasebook we had used in Temuco, Chile, memories had flooded in and she had been prompted to write. She appreciated that four years was a long time, yet she wondered if I were still looking for my paradise island because there might well be one in the Galapagos. She presumed I could afford the fare to Quito and she hoped I wasn't married! Would I please let her know immediately by telegram if I received this letter because she needed to plan the next stage in her life very soon. She had written to me twice in the first year after I left Temuco but had never received a reply.

I wondered where those letters were, for they had never caught up with me. I also wondered what I should do. This could well be the beginning of the new adventure I had been waiting for, but I was *still* thirty years older than she was, even though she was now a woman and not a university student. I decided to consult the oracle: Peter Nosworthy's lovely young wife, Julie.

Julie was a woman of the world and had known great tragedy. While serving in the QARANC she had fallen in love with a young paratrooper and married him. On the day Lord Mountbatten was blown to pieces in Northern Ireland, Julie's husband and seventeen other paratroopers were killed in similar fashion.

'Do you know what it is like to feel completely dead inside?' she'd asked me. 'That's how I was for more than a year. All I'd ever wanted out of life was to be Nick's wife.'

Through a mutual friend of Nick's she had been introduced to Peter when she had taken a job as barmaid in the Hop Pole. With his patient love and understanding she had begun to live again. Now they had a delightfully roguish little boy called Robert. I always like to think there is a rapport between Julie and me for I, too, once wore the Red Beret and I am sure that the camaraderie it carries also embraces kinfolk.

After reading Yeannie's letter, Julie told me: 'All you want me to say is that you should go – and I think you should. The memory of you must be very dear to her or she wouldn't want to keep in touch. Go and look at the Galapagos while you're down there. As Yeannie says, your paradise island could be there. You might find it together. And I wouldn't worry too much about the thirty years' difference in your ages. If she wants you and you want her, I don't think you should object. In fact, you'll be a very lucky man.'

Although Yeannie and I had changed, slightly, in the four years, we both knew when we met again in the old Inca city of Quito that the same magnetism was there. We quickly became lovers and she agreed to be my 'final' Girl Friday.

Through her friend Clarice Strang, an American nature guide on the cruise liner *Buccaneer*, we enjoyed a free 1,500-mile trip round the Galapagos. A foregone conclusion, we also fell deeply in love. As Yeannie often said: 'I think I was always waiting for you to come back to me; and possibly that is why I remained a virgin. *Why* did you have such old-fashioned ideas about my age in Temuco? We have wasted four years of delicious love-making.'

Like most people who go to 'The Enchanted Isles', Yeannie and I were charmed by the peacefulness and complete naturalness that exists on them. Yeannie loved the way we could swim in the sea with the seals which dived and swam very fast by us but never touched us. For her, the cuddly baby seals were an absolute delight. I could easily see why the Galapagos had yet another name: 'Islands Lost in Time', for all the animals and birds are as

44

tame and without fear of Man as they were in the world's beginning.

We had to step over or walk round nesting birds because they simply would not move from where they sat with eggs and young. We both burst out laughing when we first saw the huge, ludicrous chick of the albatross. It looked exactly like a cartoonist's impression of a bird that's had a hand-grenade tossed at it! 'What a mess!' I exclaimed, for the feathers, like the insides of an exploded mattress, went every which way and that.

The iguanas – sea and land species – completely ignored us as we threaded our way through hundreds of them, lying like scaly, armour-plated gargoyles on the jagged lava to soak up the sun.

Except for a poisonous apple, nothing is harmful to Man on the Galapagos – even the snakes are non-venomous, and the sharks appear to be without aggression. With snorkel and goggles a person can gaze down upon hammer-heads. On James Island, I waded into the sea where six sharks, each about two metres long, were cruising backwards and forwards in the shallows. They took no notice of me at all. We were told that there has never been a report of a shark attack in Galapagos waters.

The thirteen major islands and some fifty islets of the equatorial archipelago are the tops of giant volcanoes, rising 7,000 to 10,000 feet above the ocean floor. The build-up of the lava probably started in the Pliocene period about 10 million years ago, but the parts above the surface of the Pacific Ocean developed only during the last million years. Of particular interest to me was the discovery by scientists that the opposing directions of the lava flows showed that the Earth's magnetic lodestone had changed periodically from north to south and back again, probably causing the flooding of the world and the glaciers. I imagined the added consternation in the world today if ships' and planes' compasses suddenly showed 'north' to be in the south!

The islands also show how plants create the Earth's soil by breaking up the lava. Birds and currents bring the seeds. But, of course, the islands do not answer the age-old question: where did the first seed come from?

After a talk with the local chief of Ecuador's National Parks on Santa Cruz, the main tourist island, Yeannie and I left the *Buccaneer* to go on the local mail boat to see Isabela and Floreana islands, the only two the chief could recommend for our projects.

'Please don't ask me for permission to live on an uninhabited island,' he said, 'because I cannot give it to you.'

On the south coast of Isabela – the archipelago's largest island – was a settlement of some 400 fisherfolk. Among them, to Yeannie's delight, was a Chilean, Oscar Tricallotis, who immediately welcomed the prospect of a fellow countrywoman on the island. His wife, Lusmila Rivera – known affectionately as 'Negra' – owned 130 acres of semi-wilderness on an extinct volcano, seventeen kilometres from the sea and the village. They said we could live there, build a hut and try to farm the land. It sounded ideal.

I wanted to look at the land, but it was late at night and Yeannie and I had to be up at four the next morning to re-board the mail boat, go on to Floreana then back to Santa Cruz to rejoin the *Buccaneer*. The most important question I asked Oscar and Negra was: 'Is there fresh water on the volcano?' They assured me that there was.

Whether it was the formation of black clouds, I don't know, but Yeannie and I found the sight of Floreana Island unfriendly, in fact, sinister. As I told her, perhaps it was because we had learned, on the *Buccaneer*, a true story of a mystery on Floreana that had never been solved.

In the 1920s, a young German man took a young German woman there to live in pure existentialism – much the same sort of thing as I had been endeavouring to do on various islands. Both were from Berlin, and both were married – but not to each other. They called themselves Mr and Mrs Richter. They hadn't been on Floreana alone for very long when their solitude was invaded by another German couple called the Wittmers. After the initial re-

46

sentment on the part of the Richters, the two couples seemed to get on fairly well.

The romanticism of two couples going off to live Crusoe-style on an uninhabited island made the headlines in German newspapers. Then, just when everything seemed to be tantamount to paradise on Floreana, the Baroness arrived. She was, apparently, a real-life baroness, also German, and she had three lovers with her. According to reports, she was a sex maniac, and she wanted to be the uncrowned queen of Floreana. She always wore a pistol in her belt, and let it be known to the Richters and Wittmers that she knew how to use it. On one occasion, she shot one of her lovers in the leg. It was said that she did this so that she could nurse him and bestow upon him much love and care. Eventually, two of the lovers got fed up and left.

The Richter and Wittmer women didn't like the Baroness – possibly hated her. Reports have it that the Baroness had affairs with the Richter and Wittmer men. She was two lovers short and her sexual appetite was voracious. She was also accused of opening the Richters' and Wittmers' mail which was left in a box in the nearby bay for yachts to take.

Passing yachts also delivered mail. One day, when a yacht called in, the owner enquiring after the Baroness, she was nowhere to be found. Neither was her lover. The Ecuadorian authorities made thorough investigations, and the Richters and Wittmers appeared before a court of enquiry. Murder was an obvious possibility. Nothing was proved, and the Baroness and her lover were never seen or heard of again. A little later, Richter died on Floreana of meat poisoning.

Two books, very conflicting, were written by Mrs Richter and Mrs Wittmer, the latter's describing Richter's dying act as reaching for his wife's throat with both hands. Mrs Richter's description of the death-bed scene was of her husband reaching out to give her a last embrace. With the publication, in German, of the two books, people began wondering whether Mrs Richter had poisoned her

47

husband because he had not lived up to the original dream of romantic existentialism. Another question asked was why hadn't the Richters and Wittmers searched for the Baroness and her lover after learning they were no longer on the island.

The sole survivor is Mrs Wittmer – Margaret Wittmer – who is in her eighties and still lives on Floreana. Yeannie and I met her, but had no chance to talk to her. In any case, she prefers to speak in German. People say that if she does know what really happened she may disclose it on her death-bed.

Back on the *Buccaneer*, Yeannie and I agreed that Floreana was definitely not the choice. We would have a go at the 'farm' on Isabela. I knew it wouldn't exactly be Robinson Crusoe, but there was certainly adventure and a challenge.

During the voyage back to Guayaquil, Ecuador's main port, I told Yeannie about my promise to Rory and Redmond. 'Good,' she said. 'I want to meet them – and I think they will be very necessary to help us on the volcano.'

The day was fast approaching when Yeannie would become illegal in Ecuador because of the time limit. I decided that when I was in London for the publication of my book *The Islander* I would see the Ecuadorian Consul about her – and get visas for all of us.

With the usual red tape – and certain air of not really wanting to help unless there's money in it – that I had always encountered in embassies, the Consul wanted a letter from Oscar's wife, giving us permission to live on her land. 'But that will take weeks – even months!' I expostulated. 'You know your postal system is not exactly the best in the world.' Oscar had told us that sometimes it took a month for a letter to reach him from the mainland. 'You have my credentials. You know I want to write a book about the Galapagos. Why can't you give us visas?'

'I am sorry,' he said. 'But you can stay there for six months on your British passports. That should be sufficient time for you to write a book.'

'And what about Miss Ackermann?' I asked.

Once again the Consul expressed sorrow. There was nothing he could possibly do about her situation. So, as has often been the case in my life, I decided to say balls to bureaucracy. I was determined to live on Isabela with Yeannie, and not only because newspapers and radio stations all over Britain had announced I was going there with my new Girl Friday. The more I thought of her and me, with the two boys, conquering the wilds of Sierra Negra Volcano, the more enamoured I became by the idea. I doubted if it would be the true desert isle paradise – except that Yeannie and I would be together – for the Galapagos islands are too lava-strewn and barren on the shores for the common concept of the palm-swaying dream.

There was, too, the other idea I had, and which the boys and Yeannie liked the sound of: build a boat on the island and sail it back to England. And that could well be the answer to Yeannie's problem. The only time the authorities would know she was illegal was when she handed in her passport for stamping on leaving the country. We could build our boat in six months, and Isabela was remote enough for us to sail quietly away, with no one being the wiser.

The boys quite liked Yeannie when they met her in Quito. Naturally she was nervous and had taken great pains with her dress and make-up. They also liked Quito, for it is a very clean city. I had said nothing to them about Yeannie's position in Ecuador, and that was a mistake.

When we got to Isabela two shocks awaited us: although the volcano was lush with fruit, there was no fresh water! We had to pay for it to be delivered by tanker every week. Also, every tree was protected, even in the 'inhabited zone'. No felling allowed. All timber was brought by ship, 600 miles from the mainland – and it cost a fortune. On top of which, the local authorities demanded that we worked to one of their specified boat plans. Terribly disappointed we nonetheless decided to make a go of the farming project.

However, a few days before Christmas we received another blow – the local police suddenly arrived at our camp and asked to see our passports. Not only did they point out, politely, that Yeannie was completely illegal and had to leave the island immediately, but the boys and I, too, were also illegal.

With all the preparations and buying of equipment and provisions in Quito, I had completely forgotten to get our own passports re-stamped! The boys were immediately angry and disappointed, and blamed everything on Yeannie. While the police were examining our camp and vegetable garden, seemingly with nods of approval, I told the boys to shut up and calm down. I would get a letter from Negra, giving us permission to live there, go to Guayaquil with Yeannie, talk to the authorities and get our passports re-stamped. It was silly for all of us to pay fares. The police agreed to this. They said there was a cattle boat leaving that night, and Yeannie and I had to be on it.

So it was that we spent our first Christmas together, sharing a hard iron deck with stinking and dying cattle, pigs and goats. The voyage took six days, and for the discomfort we had to pay 90 US dollars each. The food, too, was disgusting – mostly rice and beans. The captain was permanently pissed. He told us that if he stopped drinking, the muck that the cook served up gave him a gut ache!

After a much-wanted shower, I left Yeannie in our hotel room in Guayaquil and took all our passports to the immigration authorities. The captain of police was smart in appearance but automaton in movement. First he read Negra's letter, then held out his hand for the passports. I withheld Yeannie's. 'I will give you three months more,' he said, bluntly. 'You must apply again if you want more time.' He stamped each one. I passed Yeannie's to him without comment. He read through it, appeared to be horrified and tossed it across the desk to me. 'Not possible,' he said. 'There is nothing I can do. It is possible, if she pays a lot of money, for a solicitor to legalise her, or she must pay a large fine when she leaves Ecuador.'

'How much to legalise her?' I asked.

'I think about 80,000 sucres,' he said, 'and the application would take time.'

As I walked back to the hotel, weighing both sides of the coin and finding one side loaded with £600 for legalisation, time and re-application for us – plus the regulations for boat building and extortionate cost of timber – I decided to draw stumps on the Galapagos adventure. In the hotel, I wrote a letter to the boys, telling them so. 'I will telephone England for more money and send it to you for your fares. Look after yourselves. I'll see if I can find another place to build our boat.' I put the Quito address of Lucho and Ana Fiallos at the top of the letter. They were close friends of Yeannie and we were always welcome to stay at their house. I also sent the boys a telegram, saying Yeannie couldn't return to Galapagos, letter following.

A week later I sent them, by registered post via the local airline, cash and a cheque for £50 made payable to Oscar for his kindness and any money he may have lent the boys. That letter and the telegram never reached them.

5

Rory's Diary

December 31, 1984 (Orwell's year). It all started when we brought the letter from London to dad. Now, I'm sitting on a bloody big lump of lava, thousands of miles from anywhere – all because Dad wanted to live with Yeannie. It's New Year's Eve and when I've finished this, I'm off down to the village for a piss-up with Oscar. I don't want to write this, but Redmond has already been writing his (diary), so I suppose I'd better cos Dad said I should.

Nothing has gone right since we left England on November 15. For a start, the plane from London to Amsterdam was delayed by fog and we missed the connecting DC-10 to Quito. Had to sleep in the airport lounge in Amsterdam and get on another plane, to Lima, Peru, next morning.

Because of excess weight and head winds, the plane made a four-hour detour to some little airport in the Atlantic Ocean to refuel.

In Lima, four hours late, we found that to fly to Quito would cost £160 each, and we didn't have that sort of money because Dad's money had been sent to a bank in Quito.

There was no alternative but to face a 26-hour coach journey through Peru's hot, coastal desert, on a road full of craters.

At the Peru–Ecuador border we had trouble with the guards because they had never seen an air rifle like ours before.

At Machala airport, a few miles inside Ecuador, we found that all planes to Guayaquil were fully booked, so Dad, cursing like mad, grabbed a taxi. Four and a half hours later we got to Guayaquil airport where the Quito plane was about to take off. We were rushed across the tarmac and just managed to get on board.

Two days late, we finally reached Quito – and I met Yeannie for the first time. I thought she was quite a nice person.

Back in Guayaquil – with a pile of equipment and provisions we had bought in Quito – we received another blow. Clarice and the English purser, Claiborne Mitchell, who had befriended Dad and Yeannie before, had both left the *Buccaneer*. The owners would take only writers and scientists free of charge. So Dad had to fork out special half-fares for us lot, totalling £345.

Then, when we finally got to this heap of rock – after an 85-mile trip from Santa Cruz with the locals spewing everywhere – we found there was no fresh water. To crown it all, Dad had made a complete cock-up with visas and passports – and just when we thought we were going to have a nice Christmas together, the police ordered him and Yeannie back to the mainland. I feel quite miserable. I'm off to the village. I think Dad's a fool to spend all this money because of her. Probably that's all she wants him for – to get her out of an illegal situation.

January 1. Woke up with one hell of a hangover. Went hunting with Oscar's rifle. Shot a wild donkey – that means donkey for a week. Bloody thing had four bullets in it but wouldn't die, so cut its throat. Thought again, what the hell am I doing here?

January 2. Had donkey for breakfast. Put up an aerial. Now the radio won't work at all. Everything has gone rotten with mould. Had donkey for dinner. Farted. Nearly killed myself with the stench.

January 3. Made chips – or tried to. The oil got too hot and when I took the lid off it went up in flames. Put the lid back on and all the handles melted. When the flames were out, looked in the pan and the oil was like tar. Can't

53

clean the pan. Smoking a cigarette and thinking this is the worst place I've been to. No water, not even when it rains and the temperature is between 20 and 25 degrees on this mountain and 35 in the village. We should have read more about these islands before coming here. I thought it was going to be like Cocos Island.

[I had taken all three of my sons to Cocos, a really lush tropical island about 300 miles north of the Galapagos, six years before when they were still at school.]

January 4. Dad has been gone for two weeks now and we can't even build a decent house because of lack of equipment. Went on a duck hunt with some friends of Oscar, which is strictly illegal because ducks are protected by the Parks. We got six and it was the best food I've eaten here. Went to someone's birthday party, got as pissed as a rat, fell asleep, got up and came back here in the morning. There was no mail on the boat. It's all lost somewhere, I think. The next boat is in 15 days' time.

January 5. Did nothing but eat and sleep all day. Sun is very hot. Don't know when Dad will return. We are broke but I know we can borrow money from Oscar. Might go crazy if I have to stay here another month. The girls are the worst things I've seen for years. The only nice ones are married. I think everyone here is a reject from the real world. There were some really nice girls on the mainland, but that's no good because I'm here! Don't know why, after all the time I've been here, but today I have been bitten by mosquitoes on my legs. Isn't that strange?

January 6. The bony old cow someone gave us when we first arrived because he couldn't be bothered to milk it himself, has buggered off. I don't care, it was half wild and we had to tie its head to one tree and its back legs to another to stop it kicking hell out of us when we milked it. Dad is used to milking cows but I'm not. There is only powdered milk which has gone like rock, so I'm drinking my coffee black. Redmond has gone to the village so have not spoken to anyone today. Sometimes it's so quiet I can hear myself think. Then I have to turn my mind off in case I deafen myself. Then I start talking to myself which is a sign of going nuts.

January 9. For three days have eaten spaghetti with onions and Oxo cube, washed down with freshly-squeezed orange juice. Decided to go on a chicken hunt – found nothing so we climbed an orange tree to have a look round. As we were eating oranges up in the tree, a massive cockerel came into the clearing. Redmond promptly put a shot into it, but it ran off into the bushes. We tracked and chased it for half an hour. It ran into an old shack that looked as if it hadn't been lived in for some time, and I made a mental note to go back there and steal the roof. As the cockerel ran back out through the door I shot it dead. It was a bit rubbery, but with chips and orange juice was delicious. Went to bed with full stomach and slept like a log.

January 10. Dad's tomatoes are about three inches high and doing very well in this heat. They were grown from a tomato Dad found in the road near Oscar's house and he had dried the seeds. The cabbages have come through but there's no sign of the sprouts. A few of the potatoes have also come up. We've now eaten two bunches of bananas and waiting for another load to ripen.

January 11. Redmond came back from the village and told me about Oscar catching a two-metre hammerhead on a 90lb line and a very small hook. Took 15 – 20 minutes to bring the thing in. It didn't taste like shark meat, but really nice. Negra had cooked it in batter.

January 12. After a lot of searching because there were no paths, we found the hut with a lot of tin on the roof. We also bumped into the owner! Bang goes that plan out of the window. It wouldn't do for him to come home and find his roof missing . . . Heard today that one person on the island doesn't want gringos living here. He was the one who asked the police to investigate us.

January 13. The water lorry came this morning, so I emptied all the old water out of the tank which had little worms and all sorts of other things in it. The tank holds about 70 gallons which cost about 20 pence.

January 14. Walked to the small store a kilometre away and bought some bread with money Oscar lent us. The store has run out of cigarettes. Will have to go to the village for some. Walked along the perimeter of Oscar's land. Soil is very fertile but a hell of a lot of scrub has to be cleared before anything can be planted. This part used to be farmed years ago, but the scrub kept coming back and the people gave up. Wouldn't be surprised if everybody here on the volcano gave up. It's little more than scratch farming like in the Berwyn Mountains of Wales, and most people are scared that the volcano will erupt one day. The one on Fernandina Island, only a few miles away, did last year on April 1.

January 15. Rained last night and all today. Stayed in bed. Feel depressed. Redmond returned from village with porridge and a can of tomatoes. People don't know if the cargo boat that's due tomorrow will have any cigarettes or food on board. I think they are all stupid. A native said that they are all 100 years behind the rest of the world.

January 16. Went to village. No cargo boat.

January 17. Mail boat arrived. Still no news of Dad. Got very drunk on whisky and rum.

January 18. Ill all morning. Ate nothing. A letter from Dad *was* on board. Handed to us this afternoon. It's taken more than three weeks to get here. Also received Christmas cards and letters from England. Now heard that

56

the next boat will be here in seven days. We'll leave on that. Hope the captain will accept a cheque!

January 19. Still ill.

January 20. Been thinking. Oscar will be very happy when Dad's second letter arrives with the money. Still, we can now borrow money off Oscar for our fares from Guayaquil to Quito. Walked to the top of the volcano – fantastic view. It could be good living here, but I doubt if we could build our boat. Too many rules and regulations. The land is very bad to walk on at the top. Dense jungle, and some of the craters are covered with vegetation. Started to pack our things because no one knows if the boat will be here in five days or two. Why don't they radio to find out? No cigarettes for one week now. I could smoke anything.

January 21. Washed sheets. Packed suitcases.

January 22. Did nothing.

January 23. Moved everything down to Oscar's place. Don't know how he lives as he does. Chicken and ducks in the bedroom! Plus dogs and a cat. They all sleep together. On the first day we were here, Dad asked Negra where the toilet was. She pointed to a large rock about 25 yards away. For seven years they've shit behind it. The stench and flies are terrible. The boat will arrive in two days' time! Went fishing. Caught a lot of fish and a couple of sharks.

January 24. Boat arrived today. It's the same boat Dad went on so we can pay by cheque. Sat on board and watched them load the cattle. They were driven down to the beach, ropes put round their horns and they were towed, two or three at a time, by small boats with outboards to where the cargo boat lay at anchor. As this was a good quarter of a mile from the shore, the long swim

57

almost knackered the weaker ones. Then the ropes round the horns were attached to a crane and they were hauled up on to the deck. I'm sure this stretched the necks of the heavier ones. When one cow was in mid-air, the rope snapped, and dead cow was splattered all over the deck. It was scraped up and thrown overboard. I reckon if the RSPCA could see it, they would go completely ape-shit.

January 29. Another day on this stinking tub and we'll be in Guayaquil, drinking ice-cold beer. About a quarter of the animals have died, and been thrown to the sharks. They've had a good feed of beef, pork and goat. The crew will only eat one of the animals if they can kill it just before it dies. The food on board is pretty awful but at least it's better than some of the muck Redmond and I cooked on Isabela!

Redmond's Diary – sans dates

The equator runs through the northern part of Isabela, which means that most of the time it is FH. That doesn't stand for Fahrenheit. I don't think these islands are all that beautiful. The first island we called at, courtesy of the *Buccaneer*, stank like a zoo. And walking through acres of bird-, seal- and iguana-shit isn't exactly my idea of fun.

The day we arrived here has been the only day so far that it has rained. But even after a heavy downpour like that, there wasn't the slightest sign of a trickle. The air, though, is very humid. We built our house, by the side of a large banana grove, in less than a day – and not one nail or piece of string was used. It was all done by resting long saplings on top of Y-shaped poles we had cut and dug deep into the ground. The sloping roof was made of banana leaves woven and laid on top of shorter saplings crossing the longer ones. We hung blankets down as walls and partitions. We didn't need them on our beds because it was FH. Beg your pardon, we did use string to hang the blankets.

To me befell the distinguished task of building the shithouse. 'A goodly distance from the house, please, Redmond,' said Dad. So I did, with the evil thought that if someone were taken short, he or she would never make it. The bog seems to be working all right – except I always get the nasty sensation that a fly is going to zoom up my arse. Also, I wait for the day when a piece of wood breaks and someone comes back covered from head to foot and steaming.

As there is nothing better to do, I've been trying to study electronics, but as the book I am reading is used for university bods and seems to be full of very complex chapters, I haven't a fucking clue what it's all about – which is why I am writing this crap.

Beds and tables, etc., are being built at the rate of one a day. On average, I suppose, I spend about 16 hours-plus a day in bed, only getting up to eat, shit, build something – if I've got any energy left – or re-make my bed when the sticks holding my mattress fall from under me. This generally only happens when I move.

The mosquito net surrounding my bed seems to keep more of the bastards in than out. I wouldn't mind so much if they stayed still and stopped dive-bombing my head, which causes problems when it comes to squashing them.

The stove we bought in Quito only took five days to start working, the reason being that Dad insisted we used paraffin, not petrol. After a lot of scientific experiments I discovered that paraffin needs a lot more heat to turn it into gas, otherwise it just gives off a thick, black vapour – the stove floods itself and the surrounding area; and when that catches fire everything is cremated.

* * *

I reckon, with a bit of luck, we could be off the Galapagos within three months. I think it's a nice enough place; in fact, I wouldn't mind staying here if it weren't for the water situation. In my opinion, the best thing we can do is build a boat – which was one of our main objectives – and go and find a similar place, but with a river. Cocos was the ideal place, but to live there we'd need a good boat. If we do build one and Costa Rica will give us permission, I should like to live there for a while. Would like to see how our coconuts and bananas are doing, the ones we planted in Chatham Bay.

I think today is December 15. If it is, then I've lost five days somewhere. This morning I dug a bloody big hole in an optimistic attempt to find water. We've now got a six-foot-by-three hole in our front garden with sod-all in it. Mind you, I can think of a very good use for it, if Yeannie doesn't stop rabbiting on!

The only animals we are being pestered by so far are the wild cattle and donkeys. We don't notice them so much in the day, but in the night they are all around the house, munching banana leaves for the water content and trying to reach our bunches of bananas we have hung by ropes in a tree to ripen. When a donkey decides that he is constipated and lets out an agonising and blood-curdling scream in the dead of the night, then I reckon that everyone else around has a very sudden clear-out instead!

One night we awoke to the sound of grunts of anger from a very large cow which could almost reach our banana bunches. Dad rushed out, bollock-naked, with the air rifle, and roaring: 'I'll give you something to grunt about . . . Aw! Shit!' He was correct, too. The cow had dropped a large, wet one – and Dad had put his foot in it. Because he couldn't use our precious drinking water we had fetched from the village in canisters, he had to wipe his foot in the grass. I felt quite sorry for Yeannie when she complained that he stank the bed.

* * *

60

Since Rory shot a hen on the second day, there hasn't been a single one around the area. As we later found out, many of the animals are owned by someone, which probably means that one of the farmers is a chicken short! The thing is that all the animals seem to be everywhere except where they should be, and the wild intermingle with the domesticated. This could make it very easy to swipe one – which we did – and no one would know.

Whoops! Shouldn't have written that the only animals pestering us were cattle and donkeys – rats came raiding last night, just like they did on Cocos. Tried shooting them, but it's too difficult in the starlight. Dad suggested I tried the torch along the side of the barrel. It really works! The rats always appear first in the tree next to our house in which we hang the bananas. Surveying the scene from aloft, as it were. Then down they come to eat the avocados. That's all they seem to like. Using the torch, I shot a large rat off a branch. The pellet went into the rat's earhole, mixed brains with innards and came out by the opposite back leg. All the other rats disappeared. Next night I waited until they came down from the tree and were eating the avocados. I got one on the ground and two more after they had fled to the tree. The next night I got two more. On the fourth night I was feeling too tired to wait for them to come down from the tree. I shot one off a branch. It gave a short, sharp yelp and plummeted to the ground. I memorised where it had fallen and went to sleep. Next morning we all searched for it, but never found it.

The rats have apparently got the message, for, so far as I know, they haven't been back since.

Today is Christmas Eve and there aren't any signs of snow. In fact, it's been the hottest day yet on top of this lump of lava. Haven't felt much like writing for several days. Dad and Yeannie left two days ago – all because Dad's so in love with her he doesn't know his arse from his elbow. This is my loneliest Christmas ever and somehow I don't think the presents are going to come piling in. I was told there was a letter from England for me, and I was a bit disappointed when I found out it wasn't from Leisa but from my bank.

The radio is working better with an aerial but it still needs a taller one. Not that it's worth it – Spanish carols, American news and politics and other crap like that. What *am* I doing here, stuck on top of a volcanic mountain which, with my luck, will probably erupt any minute, drinking a glass of Dad's not-quite-ready home-made orange wine, and not being able to finish writing what I want to say because there's no pissing light left?

Good morning and Merry Christmas. That's a joke for a start. It doesn't even feel the slightest bit like Christmas. And why should it? I don't believe in him, anyway.

Right! Back to where I left off when the sun disappeared. While all this bad news is happening to me I could be having a nice snuggle, watching a decent film – even *The Wizard of Oz* would seem good right now – and drinking a real pint. I was all set to go to the village this morning and go hunting, but the bus never turned up. Did I say bus? It's a creaking old lorry with seats bolted on to the front half and the back is for animals – and me when the front part's full – fruit, tools and anything else. If things keep going as they are, I think I shall go back to England for my birthday in March.

For the first week we were here, we had a near-neighbour: Gustavo and his wife and kids. After only two months they had decided it was too harsh a life to try farming there and had gone back to Ecuador. They'd told people in the village they were only going for a few weeks for Christmas. But they'd told us they were never coming back. I only mention this because some bod just arrived and handed me a small package to look after until Gustavo and family return.

This bag of goodies contains a load of sweets from a school in Ecuador for Gustavo's kids. I said I would look after them. It's like a Christmas present from heaven. What a bastard I am!

62

It's coming to the end of Christmas Day and there's only a few minutes of light left. So far today I've walked to the local shop, had two craps, and spent the rest of the day in bed, pigging those revolting sweets.

It is now Boxing Day. Yippee! And, as they say on Radio Wyvern for the weather report: 'It's rainin'.'

It rained all that day and night, and the next day and night. All this time I've been lying in bed, reading *King Rat*.

I have just finished the book this morning, the 28th. The sky is completely filled with clouds. Today I saved a Darwin Finch from drowning. She was in our large water tank and couldn't get out. I put her by the fire to dry out her wings. Then the silly sod lost her balance and fell into the flames. No damage was done – just a new pattern on her right wing. I wrapped her in a blanket and fed her some flies. About an hour later she tested her wings and, after a little hesitation, took off.

For a change, ate donkey today after Rory slaughtered it. Tasted like pure rubber. Oscar told us that donkey meat always gives a person violent wind with unbearable stench. I'll say! One fart and I massacred all the mozzies inside my mosquito net. Which didn't do any good because I had to get out of bed immediately so that I wouldn't be gassed, and more of the little bastards flew in.

Spent a really nice day, fishing with Oscar and his younger brother, David, who only arrived recently from Chile. I used Dad's 'White Hunter' knife, made by Puma and donated to him by Whitby & Co of Cumberland. Oscar and David were quite impressed by the way the knife sliced through the sandpaper skin of the sharks and immediately wanted to buy it. I told them it wasn't for sale. They kept pestering me for it, so I shan't take it to the village again. When I told Rory about it, he said that

63

the men on the donkey hunt had wanted to buy the Bowie knife he had used and which had also been sent to Dad by Whitby. We decided to put them in the bottom of one of the suitcases for safety.

It's like being in the doldrums with no news of Dad. They say there's been a total strike in Quito, mailmen and all. That's another bloody thing that's gone wrong. Sometimes I think that Yeannie is a jinx.

Rory has been writing his diary, so that gives me a good excuse for getting a severe attack of writer's cramp!

Decided to write again today because, after what seems like six years, we are back again in civilisation in steaming Guayaquil. Have just spoken to Dad on the phone. He's flying down to pay our fares to Quito. The money we borrowed from Oscar went on a giant piss-up in Santa Cruz after we met an Aussie called Steve on the cattle boat. Joy of joy – Dad's found us another place to build our boat. We're all off to the wilds of Colombia. Who am I kidding? If Yeannie's had anything to do with it, it's bound to be another balls-up.

6

I enjoyed reading the boys' accounts of the Galapagos adventure and laughed a lot at some of their expressions. I liked the way they had obviously conferred so as not to duplicate and I thought they had presented quite an accurate picture. I told them so, adding that perhaps they, too, could be writers – if they put their minds to it.

All Sunday afternoon we spent cleaning utensils and packing everything except for what we needed that night. 'I'm getting a bit tired of doing this,' said Redmond. 'You didn't have to do it on the Galapagos.'

'Never mind,' I said, 'we'll only have seven pieces because we're not taking provisions. That's two less than we had to pack in Quito. It will balance us nicely – two each for us three and one plus beloved coffee plant for Yeannie.'

When Yeannie and I went to say *adios* to Mercedes and Tia Maria that evening we also called in at the shop to say goodbye. 'Please come round at eight tomorrow morning,' said the shop woman, 'for coffee and a little present for you to remember us by.'

We did so, and Yeannie chatted with her over coffee. Her name was Señora Amparo. Once more she said she would be sorry to see us go and gave Yeannie a shopping bag, hand-woven in many colours.

Like the old 'dog kennel' woman, Yeannie had gathered wild plants and put them in a variety of containers to decorate the house. These she gave to the old woman, much to that old soul's intense gratitude.

The locals' idea of a Pullman coach and ours didn't quite coincide, though it did have a conductor as well as driver.

'How much is the fare to Tumaco?' Yeannie asked him as our luggage was being stowed in compartments along the side and at the rear of the dust-covered vehicle.

'I don't know,' he said. 'Better ask the conductor.'

'Here we go again,' I said to her. 'Think of a number and double it.' Of course he knew what the fare was, but he and the conductor would use each other for courage to extract as much money from us as possible. This sort of thing goes on all over the world.

When the conductor came up, the driver asked him pointedly, what the Tumaco fare was. 'You should know,' was the reply. 'You have it written down somewhere.'

'No, you have it,' said the driver. They both made ineffectual searches through papers. While the farce was going on we were being appraised by a bus-load of impatient eyes. The driver, after a nod of encouragement from the conductor, blurted out: '750 pesos.'

Yeannie decided that a lie was in order. 'No it isn't. The *alcalde* told us we shouldn't pay more than 500.'

'Prices have gone up,' said the conductor. '650.'

'We can only afford 600,' said Yeannie.

'All right,' said the conductor, grudgingly, and he took the money. I noticed that we didn't get tickets.

Only the back row wasn't occupied, so we had no choice of seats – and no springs or cushions! But there was stuffing of sorts under the plastic covers which took some of the shock when the back wheels thudded down into the pot-holes.

Pususquere lies about 150 miles north of the equator, but its altitude of some 6,000 feet keeps the temperature down a little. But the lower down the winding road we went, the hotter it became. More windows were opened and more dust came in. It seemed to prefer the back of the bus. By mid-day, when we stopped at a restaurant in a small town, the vegetation was very thick and bananas were everywhere. The driver had parked on the side of the dirt road, and when we returned after lunch the near-side wheels had sunk to their axles in the wet earth. For nearly an hour we waited until a suitable vehicle was found to tow us out.

Forty-five minutes later, when our bladders were being pressured, the driver stopped again and everybody rushed

66

out, obviously all with full bladders. The Colombian women *squatted* next to the coach but the negresses just lifted their skirts, dropped their colourful knickers and pissed standing up like the men. Yeannie was the only woman who sought seclusion. She and I went behind a convenient rock. 'Very interesting,' commented Rory, when we were back in our seats. 'There's quite a flood around the coach.'

'Yeah,' said Redmond. 'Probably the wheels will sink again!'

The next stop was an enforced one late in the afternoon and was quite alarming. The heat was tropical and we were in the middle of miles and miles of dense jungle. A band of guerrilla-like figures, armed with sub-machine guns, suddenly appeared, spread across the road in front of us. The driver braked to a halt. An order was given and we all had to get off the coach. 'Dick Turpin in multiplication,' said Redmond.

The women were waved to one side by the sub-machine guns and I caught the fear and alarm in Yeannie's eyes as she was forced to go with them. All the men were then lined up, facing the side of the coach with arms raised and hands resting on it. While one group covered us with the guns, another came behind, kicked our legs apart and roughly searched us. I couldn't say for sure whether they were legitimate troops or bandits. They wore blue berets and jungle camouflage smocks similar to Denisons worn by British paratroops.

The boys and I were at the end of the line. I reasoned that I hadn't heard a gun being cocked or a safety catch being slipped, both ominous clicks at close range, and I knew from experience that the only time military-trained personnel carried a weapon at the ready was when an attack or ambush was imminent. Not even in the front line of Korea did we walk about with rifles cocked and safety catches off.

If I heard a click, I knew precisely what I would do, as I had been trained to do when an armed enemy was standing too close for his own safety – get behind or level

67

with the gun muzzle; in this case by diving for the legs of the man immediately behind me, and shouting to Rory and Redmond to do the same. With the element of surprise we could snatch their guns away and shoot as many of the bastards as possible.

But it didn't happen. A man who had the bearing and command of an officer – though no insignia to prove it – approached me and asked for our passports. To my relief, he told me they were Marine Commandos. I told him that the passports were in a grip among the luggage. He ordered the conductor to open the compartment and they went through all our bags that were in there. Luckily, the knives and air rifle were in the rest of our luggage in the back of the coach. Satisfied that we were all in order, he called off his dogs and disappeared into the jungle.

'More incidents like that,' said Redmond, 'and I think I shall age very quickly.'

'What you need, my lad,' I said, 'is three years' service in the Paras.'

'And get a bullet in my back in Northern Ireland?' he retorted. 'Bollocks!'

Rory said nothing, but I saw that the muscles above his very strong jaw-line were twitching. 'When they lined you up along the side of the coach,' said Yeannie, 'I thought I would shit myself. I thought they were going to shoot you.'

'Yes,' I said, 'the St Valentine's Day Massacre did cross my mind.'

'What is that?' she asked. I let Redmond explain.

The fourth and final stop before we reached Tumaco was also compulsory. A huge gravel lorry had broken down alongside a giant mound of gravel that had been deposited to mend the road. The sun had dipped, and in stark relief against the crepuscular sky we could see three men with shovels on top of the mound, trying to dissipate and flatten it. Behind were the lights of other waiting vehicles.

'Let's get out of this tin oven and stretch our legs,' said Rory. That was when we met 'Señor Brandy'. We called him that because of the bottle he carried. 'Havva drink,' he said, in English, by way of greeting. We all accepted. He wore horn-rimmed spectacles and was so round-shouldered, weedy and tall that I thought a puff of wind could knock him over. Balancing his round shoulders was a stomach that shot out from under sunken chest as though he had a football down the front of his trousers. He looked like a cartoonist's caricature of himself.

In a mixture of Spanish and bad English he told us he represented the local roads authority. 'This sort of thing is always happening,' he said, 'because the bloody people are stupid.'

'Are there many white people in Tumaco?' asked Yeannie. 'And tourists?'

He laughed a waft of brandy fumes into our faces. 'There are only two white people in Tumaco,' he said, 'a Canadian and an American. My dear, there are no tourists in Tumaco any more. The port has been closed for a long time. The place is crawling with negroes. That's why I drink this stuff. Have another.' He once more handed us the bottle.

'And banks?' asked Yeannie, taking a swig. 'Ooh! I feel drunk!'

'There are a couple of banks,' said Señor Brandy, 'but they are only small branches.'

Yeannie explained about our finances. 'You have personal English cheques?' he asked. I told him yes.

'Then the only thing for you to do is open an account with a cheque because they will not change pounds. They will send the cheque to England and in about twenty-one days you will have your pesos. Excuse me.' He took back his now quite depleted bottle. 'I have to see what those idiots are going to do about the lorry. I think the gravel will be low enough to pass over soon, though.'

On empty stomachs the brandy had bestowed upon us rose-tinted spectacles – we were peacefully resigned to whatever Tumaco had in store. I had even forgotten to ask Señor Brandy another important question. For the past five miles or so we had passed through what was tantamount to ribbon development in the most rustic

69

sense: small, elongated villages with wooden huts – not houses – along each side of the road and negroes sitting outside them. In each village had been a larger hut bearing a red cross on a white background with the words 'Malaria Zone – Dispensary'.

'That's all we bloody well need,' Rory had said.

It was pitch black when we got on the move again. But the moon was shining an hour later when we reached the outskirts of Tumaco. We passed by a string of large timber yards next to the water's edge, crossed a small bridge and went down an unlit street with continuous rows of wooden huts on either side and candles flickering inside them. Supreme optimists, we eagerly waited for the centre of the town to start with concrete buildings, hotels and shops. Alas, there was no centre as such. The huts did change into buildings – two-storeyed at that – but all was wood. And still no street lights.

The bus stopped in a busy street with people walking up and down, and candle-lit pavement stores still open although it was close to eleven o'clock. Outside a fresh fish shop, a negro sat with a shotgun across his lap. We were told it was the end of the line – and it certainly seemed like it. The air stank of a mixture of pigs, fish and rotting vegetables. From what we could see of the street, it was littered with garbage. Half-naked men jostled by us as we waited for our luggage. The brandy had left our stomachs a bit raw; we felt hungry, tired and depressed. Yeannie asked the conductor if he could recommend a hotel, if such a thing existed there. 'All hotels that way,' he said, dismissing us and pointing up the street to where it dissolved into darkness.

'Dad,' said Rory, grimly, 'this place is worse than Pususquere.'

'It's only because we're tired and hungry, and it's dark,' I told him, not believing a word I said.

'It's a shit-hole, Dad,' said Redmond, firmly. 'And you know it. What a stench!'

'Well, we'll have to get a hotel,' I said. 'We can't do

anything else, and we'll see what it's like in the morning.'

'Yes, but who's ever heard of a bloke sitting outside his shop with a shotgun?' Rory wanted to know.

'And I'm sure I can smell human shit,' added Redmond.

'I can, too,' said Yeannie.

'I must admit,' I said, as we were deciding who would carry what, 'I would feel a lot happier if I had the White Hunter stuck inside my belt.'

Two negro youths, wearing only trousers and shoes and pushing an empty barrow, came up to us. 'You want a hotel?' one asked. His Spanish had a marked Afro-Caribbean accent. 'Yes,' said Yeannie.

'We take you to a good hotel.' They began putting our luggage on to the barrow 'Hey, wait a minute,' I said, 'we have no money until the banks open tomorrow. And how much does the hotel cost?'

'That's OK. The woman is very nice – you won't be molested in this hotel. It costs only 200 pesos a day.'

'All right,' I said. 'Let's go and have a look at it.' Off we set along the moonlit street in the direction the conductor had indicated, the two young men taking turns to push the heavy load. After fifty yards or so we turned off the street into a darker one because the buildings obscured the moon.

'Where the hell are they taking us?' Rory demanded.

'Probably to have our throats cut,' I said. To the two men, I added: 'Exactly where is this hotel?'

One pointed ahead. 'Not far,' he assured us. A minute or so later we arrived at a locked door with a sign above which we couldn't read. One of the youths rang the bell, and after a while we heard footsteps approaching. Bolts were slid back, a key was turned and there stood a pleasant-faced, young Colombian man holding a candle. We could see that the building was partly cement and it looked quite clean. Yes, he had rooms. Please bring the luggage inside. After everything had been carted up a flight of stairs to the reception area, I asked our two helpers how much for their trouble.

'1,000 pesos,' said one of them.

71

'Don't be bloody silly,' I exclaimed. 'A taxi wouldn't have cost anywhere near that amount.'

'It was a lot of hard work, pushing the barrow,' he said, hotly. 'And we have found you a nice hotel. We want 1,000 pesos.'

I turned to the Colombian. 'Where is the woman who owns this hotel?'

'Just tell them to piss off, Dad,' said Rory. 'We're not paying 1,000 pesos.'

'Just hang on a minute,' I told him. 'Let's get the woman here. She'll know how much we should pay. The last thing I want is bad feelings here on our first night.'

The Colombian led us up more stairs to the flat roof on which cabins had been built. One of them was well-lit with a pressure lamp. The woman inside was about forty and greeted us warmly. Yeannie told her that we only had English money and that the two youths wanted 1,000 pesos for bringing our luggage from where the bus had stopped.

Señora de Lopez, as she had introduced herself, became instantly furious. 'You robbing bastards,' she stormed at the young men, 'with people like you here we will never get tourists. You give Tumaco a bad name.'

A furious argument ensued. 'Shut up!' the señora finally silenced them. To Yeannie she said: 'I will lend you some money – 1,000 pesos. Give these robbing bastards 500 and no more – even that is too much – then I will show you a nice restaurant where you can get a meal. It is too late to eat here.'

Yeannie took the two 500-peso notes and gave one to the growling youths. They left, shouting obscenities to us over their shoulders.

'What a lovely person,' Yeannie said, as we were eating roast chicken and chips in the friendly atmosphere of the El Pais restaurant not far from the Hotel Don Pepe. 'I suppose 500 pesos was worth it for finding her. The sheets are clean and I think we are very fortunate.' And even Rory and Redmond, with their bellies becoming rapidly full, were forced to grunt in agreement.

72

7

Tumaco stands on a small island, linked to the mainland by a bridge about forty feet long. All in all, I would say that the island's area is about one square mile, and there aren't many square yards that aren't covered by wooden huts and buildings. Some of the streets are paved, the majority, dirt.

Any person arriving at night could be readily excused for thinking that Tumaco was the dirtiest, smelliest and hottest place on earth. But in the daytime, with the sun's rays putting an eye-squinting glare on everything, that person can easily see that Tumaco *is* the dirtiest, smelliest and hottest place on earth! The whole shoreline perimeter is represented by a barrier of huts, stores, hotels and restaurants – plus a petrol station for boats – the heights of the corrugated iron roofs varying and making the skyline more ragged than architectural. Nearly all waterfront buildings extend over the sea on piles and all rubbish is slung beneath in the hope that the two-metre tide will take it away. But it doesn't – it compacts it into a solid wall of stench. At various points, as though rotting garbage and fish were insufficient to pollute the air, there is pig shit and human shit. Black pigs live *en familia* with many of the negroes in the already cramped huts, and a hole in the floorboards is the lavatory and rubbish dispenser.

In the real negro quarter on the western side, where no Colombians live, the huts along the shore are three or even four rows deep. The town council provides rubbish collection vehicles and whether it is these that keep down the amount of refuse beneath the inland huts to a thin layer, or whether most of the refuse is dumped underneath the huts actually standing in the water, I wouldn't like to say.

The first – and only time – we went there, when we had lost our way, I felt really sad that human beings could live like that.

It was our first morning in Tumaco and we were looking for an address Megaphone had given us, a friend of hers who would rent us a house. We never did find it, and, as Yeannie said: 'If it's in this district we don't want to.' There was no hope for the people there. There they would live, like bees in a swarm, until they died. 'God, Yeannie,' I said, 'in England, our animals live better than this.'

'I know,' she replied. *'El mundo es un culo.'*

'This *place* is an arsehole,' said Rory. 'The one road leading to it – which we came along – is the colon.'

'And we thought the people in Pususquere were poverty-stricken!' said Redmond. 'But I think we should get out of this quarter fast, Dad. They've all got machetes – and even that toddler there has a big knife!'

'I think you're right,' I agreed. 'We'll back-track to that big white building that said "Convent" and ask the way.'

As we walked back along the brown, barren sidewalk, strewn with bits of paper and cigarette ends, no one moved aside. They just stood and regarded us with a supercilious, mocking air. So we walked along the road.

Finding our way out of the Negro quarter back to what passed as Tumaco's main street we popped into the two banks, each one opposite the other. Neither wanted to know English pounds, and only one of them, the Republic Bank, would entertain the idea of opening an account with an English personal cheque. Even so, they didn't want my cheque because it was Bromyard, Herefordshire. 'Haven't you a London bank?' they asked.

Rory's bank was in London. 'Write a cheque to yourself for £1,000,' I told him, 'and I'll write to Mr Wilson, your loans officer, enclosing my cheque.' The Post Office next door had assured us that a letter to England would take a maximum of nine days.

When I posted the letter, I couldn't believe the cheapness of the stamp; only 32 pesos! 'Are you sure that's airmail?' I asked. The man was positive. Not only that, but the letter would get there just as fast as a certified postage one.

Comparing prices, we found that our hotel was the cheapest place to eat. Very fortunate, because we had no alternative – no pesos. We told Señora de Lopez of our predicament. 'Go and see the Father,' she said. 'He's always going to Europe.'

The priest was easy to find – he lived next door to the Catholic church, the tallest building in Tumaco. The twinkle in his blue eyes, I could have sworn, was not strictly due to celibacy. 'My English is very bad,' he apologised. 'You know Scotch? White Horse?' The white was pronounced bite. I nodded. 'Of course,' I said.

'You have some? I like very much.' It was my turn to apologise. 'Pity. Pity,' he said. 'However – what can I do for you?'

I held out six 10-pound notes. 'Can you change these?'

'Oh, a lot of money! Wait, let me see what the exchange rate is.'

'I think Father likes a tot or two,' said Rory, after the priest had left the room. We waited quite a while for his return. When he came back he had a wad of pesos in his hand. 'The exchange rate is 145,' he said. 'Here is 8,700 pesos. I am going to Spain soon, and there are always English colleagues there.' He was now speaking in Spanish, and he asked us what we were doing in Tumaco. Yeannie told him about the boat project.

'That's quite an adventure, and a very brave one,' he said. 'The waves outside this port are tremendous. Didn't you know that? It is because of the shallows. The worst place is Cape of Currents where many currents meet. You will need a guide to get you out to sea. I think you should go and see the Major of Marines, he is the best person to see for advice. The barracks are on the other island where there are the sandy beaches and a small airport. You cross the very long bridge to it.'

I asked him about timber, and he said it was very cheap. 'But,' he added, 'inspect every plank. A lot of the timber has woodworm.'

75

Next morning we took a 30-peso bus ride to the barracks, which were heavily guarded by soldiers wearing the same uniforms as those who had stopped the coach, a difference being that they had cap badges. Our passports were taken, and, after a long wait, we were escorted by two armed guards to the major's office.

He looked about thirty-five, was fresh-complexioned with sandy blond hair, and seemed delighted to see us. 'From England, eh?' he said, shaking our hands. 'Good. I can practise my English!' He was obviously showing off to two doting junior officers who positively beamed with pride at the prowess of their beloved major. What they didn't appreciate was that his English was absolutely awful.

I'd noticed that whenever the major – who was seated behind an immaculately polished desk – needed anything, he snapped his fingers and his two acolytes leapt to attention and executed his command: more chairs for us, a notepad and pen for himself, a glass of water, a light for a cigarette. They hovered, like loving, obedient dogs, for their master's orders.

Several times, the major couldn't think of a particular English word, and he snapped his fingers in an endeavour to recall it to memory. And, of course, each time he did so, his aides immediately and automatically answered the digital command by snapping to attention. And there they stood, rigid and rather bewildered, until I, obligingly, supplied the word so that they could relax, smiling again.

I knew by experience that it wasn't only discipline that made those junior officers behave like that. There was obviously respect for the man behind the uniform. Which meant that the major was quite a guy. It was evident that he enjoyed our company for we were there, talking – thankfully not all the time in English – for almost an hour. The outcome was that the major didn't care what we built, so long as it wasn't harmful to the community; but we definitely needed someone to go with us to buy the wood or we would be robbed blind.

'There's a Canadian here, a very important man. He is the director of Plan de Padrinos, the world-wide Foster

76

Parents Organisation. His name is Jerry Vink. I know him well. Wait, I will telephone him for you. Then perhaps you can meet.'

The major handed me the phone after exchanging pleasantries with the person on the other end. The voice was warmly Canadian with a slight accent I couldn't place. 'What on earth are English people doing in Tumaco?' it wanted to know.

'It's a long story,' I said.

'I'd like to hear it,' was the answer. 'Look, I always have a drink in the Oasis Bar at six o'clock in the evenings. Would you like to meet me there today?'

'Fine. Where is it?'

'Where are you staying?' he countered. I told him the Hotel Don Pepe. 'That's a nice place,' he said. 'The Oasis is not far from there.' He gave me directions, and asked to speak to the major again.

After the major had put down the phone I thanked him for his help. As we shook hands I mentioned the coach incident. 'One of our patrols,' he explained. 'A lot of – how you say, nasty? – people come to Tumaco. We have to keep a constant watch. Good luck with your venture. I'm sure Jerry will help you, and don't forget, go and see the Port Captain. He, too, is a very nice man.'

From where the bus dropped us back in the town, we had to walk down the street where the banks were. Mid-way along it, three men called out sharply to us from the other side. We ignored them. Another shout and they hurried across the road and one grabbed my arm. I was about to knock him aside when he flipped open a wallet with his other hand. 'DAS,' he said, crisply. He was an agent of Colombia's equivalent to the CIA.

Luckily, we had our passports on us. Even so, he wanted to know where we were staying, and he told us to report to his chief for further questioning at ten o'clock the following morning. A crowd of interested passers-by had gathered round, trying to peer over our shoulders as the agent read through our passports. The other two agents told them, in no uncertain terms, to clear off. The onlookers went to the other side of the street and there they stood, laughing, talking and pointing us out to others who came walking by. 'I am sorry,' said the agent. 'Please proceed.'

'Bloody hell!' Rory seethed. 'It's like being in a bloody zoo!' The high noon sun was quite vicious and the concrete and sand pavement burned through the soles of our shoes. It wasn't the most opportune of times and places to be stopped and interrogated in front of, as Redmond put it, a bunch of stupid layabouts.

Feeling better after lunch and a couple of beers, and wanting to find out about things as quickly as possible, I suggested we went to see the port captain. The boys said they'd had enough and were going to sit on the hotel's flat roof and get some sea breeze. So Yeannie and I went alone. The other island had few houses and it was peaceful and quiet.

Capitán Daniel Gutierrez and his personal secretary were two charming young men, Colombian and, like the major, in their thirties. The building, next to a high, tree-strewn rock with a lighthouse on top and the waves lapping below, was like a long, wooden bungalow. Inside, the offices were big and airy. Venetian blinds hung down the large windows. Model ships in glass cases, charts and maps lent a true nautical atmosphere. The whole place was spotlessly clean.

Yeannie and I were asked to sit on a comfortable settee in front of the captain's desk. An attractive young woman in a blue silk dress served us coffee. I let Yeannie do the talking.

'Wonderful,' said Capitán Gutierrez, when she had finished. 'You have a plan of your boat?'

'Yes,' I said, 'but it's a bit rough as yet.''

'No matter. Tell me about it.'

'Length overall, 38 feet, beam, 11-foot-6, height 8 feet,' I said.

He nodded. 'A good size. Power?' I told him sail and a small engine. 'You know these waters are terrible off this coast? In fact, they are treacherous for as far as the port of Buenaventura – that is about mid-way between here and Panama. The local people use the inland waterways that the sea has made. But they are very complex, through many islands, and you would need a guide. However, first things first – where are you going to build your boat?'

'We have to find a place,' I said. 'We are meeting a Canadian at six this evening. I am hoping he will be able to suggest something.'

'Ah, Jerry – he is a good friend of mine. Yes, I am sure he will help you. When you have built your boat it is necessary that I give you certain papers, the boat must be registered here, and you must have permission to leave and an international certificate so that you can call at other ports. But those are no problem. It would assist me to grant you those documents, though, if you had a Colombian naval architect to help you and put his name to your plan. And I have one in mind. His name is Panchano. Would you like him to call at your hotel tomorrow evening to discuss it?'

'Certainly,' I said. 'Thank you very much.'

He asked about my experience, and I told him, truthfully, that I made dug-outs with only the use of an axe, had helped build a 25-foot power boat of wood in the Torres Strait, had been in many tricky situations at sea, and had on many occasions made forty-mile trips across treacherous seas in a 14½-foot dinghy.

'Navigation?'

'A long time ago, I knew how to use a sextant. I'm sure I would soon pick it up again.'

'Good,' he said. 'I'm afraid I am going away for three weeks tomorrow, but my secretary here is a very experienced seaman, and if you have any problems, call on him.'

At five forty-five p.m. the boys, Yeannie and I set off for the Oasis Bar. We found it without difficulty. Inside, it was clean, cool and cosy, as all bars should be in hot climes. Also, the few negroes there paid little attention to us. We were drinking cold beers when a voice said: 'Well, you people certainly aren't difficult to recognise!'

Jerry Vink wore a black Vandyke beard, and with his

79

black hair and tanned face he could easily have been
Colombian. His brown eyes held compassion and his whole
face exuded friendliness. I ordered him a beer, and he
listened attentively as we all contributed to pouring out
our saga.

'It's unbelievable,' he said. 'And now here you are in
sunny Tumaco – which most people have never heard
of – with a crazy idea of building a boat and sailing to
England; on top of that, you have no money. You
English . . . !' He shook his head and chuckled with great
amusement. 'And what does the Chilean complement
think about it?' he added, in Spanish. Yeannie smiled.
'It's crazy,' she said, 'and I know I shall be frightened.
But I want to be with Gerald so I am going to do it.'

'I shall say you'll be frightened,' said Jerry. 'Wait till
you see those waves outside this port!'

Still chuckling, he called for more beers. 'What do you
think of Tumaco?' he asked.

'It is very dirty,' said Yeannie, 'and we do not like some
of the living conditions here.'

'Yes, Tumaco does have its problems,' conceded Jerry,
'but most of the people are very nice – warm and friendly
when you get to know and understand them. I've been
here nearly six years, so I should know.'

'Six years!' echoed Rory, 'I'd go nuts!'

'I drink my fair share of this . . .' holding up his glass and
smiling, '. . . and rum. In fact, I live very comfortably.'

'What exactly is Plan de Padrinos?' I asked.

'One of the founders was one of your journalists, Mal-
colm Muggeridge. It's a world-wide, sponsored organisation to help the poor and needy. We create employment,
start projects so that people can work and help themselves
– we have our own fishing fleet, for example – we provide
education and medical care.'

'Sounds pretty good,' I said. 'Speaking of medical care,
is there malaria in this area?'

'Phew! Lots of it. And typhoid. Arthur, an American
who also works here for Plan, is away sick with typhoid at
the moment. Everybody gets it.'

'Do you take prophylactic tablets for the malaria?'

'No,' he said. 'I think they weaken your resistance. Hey! Here comes my son.'

A little black boy of about five or six came running up to our table. Jerry picked him up, lovingly, and placed him on his lap.

'Your son?' queried Redmond, with marked surprise.

'Sure,' said Jerry. 'He's my very own. Carlitos, say "How do you do" to these nice people and shake their hands. They are from England – and the young lady is from Chile.'

Carlitos did so. Jerry placed 250 pesos on the table. 'That's for the beers. I have to go. I can let you have some money, that's no problem, but a house to rent . . . I'll have to think about it. See Panchano tomorrow evening – he's a nice guy – and call at my office the following morning at any time. It's simple to get to – turn left outside your hotel and keep walking for about half a kilometre until you come to a big white building on the right. Just ask anyone for me. And if you have any trouble with DAS tomorrow morning ask them to phone me. They know my number.'

'Right,' I said, after Jerry and son had left, 'let's have another round by way of celebration. I think we're doing pretty well and that Jerry is going to be a very good friend. I like him a lot.'

'Fancy having a piccaninny for a son, though,' said Rory.

I pointed out that that was Jerry's concern, not ours. I didn't say so, but I had been shocked at the arrival of Carlitos, and although I questioned myself about it, I couldn't produce a sensible answer why. That night in our hotel room, with the geckos crawling upside down across the ceiling, Yeannie told me that she didn't think it very nice for Jerry to have a black son, and she wondered where Jerry's wife was.

'I feel a fool, too,' she went on. 'I told Jerry that we didn't like the negroes in Tumaco.'

'Don't worry about it,' I comforted her. 'Stick by your principles. No one should like anyone because another

81

person says so. It's what you feel inside that counts. But that doesn't mean you shouldn't be polite. So we'll just forget it and say nothing more to him about negroes.'

The next day, after clearing things up with the DAS, we went to see Panchano. He was a big man with large, calloused hands. He'd always wanted to build a fantastic motor yacht instead of the usual trawlers, and this could be his opportunity. After looking at my rough drawings, he quickly named every type of South American wood to be used for ribs, keel, planking, deck and cabins.

'How much is this going to cost?' I asked.

'For everything, including my fee of 1,500 pesos a day, radio, sails and engine, one and a quarter million pesos,' he replied.

With pen and paper I divided that vast amount by 145. It came to £8,620! 'Isn't there a cheaper way?' I asked. He shook his head. He wasn't interested in any short cuts. Either that or nothing. He certainly wouldn't put his name to anything slipshod which used inferior timber. 'I'll have to think about it,' I told him. 'We have no money as yet until it arrives from England.'

'No problem,' he replied. 'I will buy the wood for you and you repay me later.'

'No,' I said, firmly. 'Let me get the money here first.'

He shrugged. 'OK. I will write you my address. Come to my yard any time. I am building a fishing boat at the moment.'

Just as he was leaving, I asked him how long it would take to build a boat, and he said three months.

'Could it be done in two if we all helped?'

'Oh, yes,' he said. 'No problem, but I would have to buy the timber this week.'

'The trouble is,' I explained, 'we had to see DAS this morning and we are allowed only until May 9 to stay in this country.' He calculated the time left. 'Two and a half months is fine,' he said. 'Let me know your decision quickly.'

After he'd gone, Rory asked: 'How did you calculate we could build a 25-footer for £75?'

'You saw the figures,' I said, 'and you heard what Lola's brother told me: 9' x 1' planks cost 80 pesos.'

'Yes, but Dad,' Redmond interrupted, drily, 'I think Panchano intends to use *real* wood. You know, like they make proper yachts with?'

I laughed. 'I know,' I said. 'It's a marvellous opportunity – we could probably sell it for about £25,000 or more in England – but it can't be done.'

'Why not?' demanded Rory.

'Because,' I said, 'I reckon I'm only good for £4,000. To get more I would need the bank to lend me the money; that would entail insurance and no insurance company is going to act without seeing the boat first, and God knows how long that would take. Another factor is that we would need more money than the boat costs – we have to live in the meantime, then there's fuel, port costs, especially at Panama, and provisions on board. Yet another thing, there's not much of a story in sailing to England in a de luxe yacht that someone else has built.'

'Simple solution,' said Redmond. 'Let's get Panchano to build us half a yacht! You can afford that!'

'With your brains,' I said, 'you'd probably have the deck and cabins built and no keel. No, seriously, I'm getting another idea. All these people here use dug-out canoes – now that's something we know how to build.'

'I'm not going to England on a tree trunk!' said Rory.

'Why not?' I asked. 'According to Señora de Lopez they go in the big canoes all the way down to Ecuador and back.'

'I think we should stick to our original idea of the 25-footer and build it ourselves,' said Rory. 'If it's sea-worthy, the captain will issue the documents. If it's not, I'm not getting into it!'

'All right,' I pacified him, 'but first we've got to find somewhere to live *and* to build the boat. We're not having much luck in that respect so far. Let's hope Jerry comes up with something. The hotel bill is crippling us.'

That afternoon we had followed up two leads given to us by Señora de Lopez, but one house had already been let and the other meant sharing with another family, and it was well inland. She had asked around further, but, so far as she knew, there were no other houses to let in Tumaco – at least, not suitable for us. 'There are vacant huts in the negro quarter,' she said, 'but if you lived there you would be robbed instantly, possibly killed.'

When we called in on Jerry the next morning, we found that the premises of Plan de Padrinos were quite extensive and housed inside a high brick wall. People hustled and bustled everywhere. There were admin offices, a wood and paint shop, a blacksmith and a medical section with a queue of pregnant women and others with babies waiting to see the doctor. The large white, cement building was a co-operative store.

We were told that Señor Vink's office was in the central building. The clack of typewriters greeted us as we entered. Large ceiling fans whirled above the several desks in the reception area. Attractive black girls in variegated summer dresses stopped hammering away at the typewriters and smiled at us. One got up and approached us. 'You wish to see Señor Vink?' she asked. 'One moment, please.'

Jerry's office was the end one leading off the reception area. It was large with comfortable seating and cooled by two electric wall fans. Jerry's desk was polished wood and everything upon it was immaculately placed. On the wall behind his chair was a large, framed plaque from the Municipality of Tumaco, honouring Jerry's five year's service to the community.

'Quite a busy place,' I commented. Jerry was engrossed with a mains electric calculator. 'Hi!' he greeted us. 'Have a seat. I am doing the year's accounts and I seem to have lost five million pesos somewhere.' He pushed the calculator aside. 'No doubt I'll find them. How are things going with you people?'

I told him not very well, that DAS wanted us out of Colombia by May 9 and that Panchano wanted a million and a quarter pesos to build our boat. 'That's very cheap,' he said. 'You don't think so? How much were you thinking of spending?'

'£75,' I said.

'Are you serious? Do you know how much a dug-out canoe costs here? Nearly £400. You *are* serious!' And he laughed uproariously. 'My friend,' he went on, 'if you can build your boat for £75 I will buy you a bottle of Scotch.'

'You're on,' I said. And we shook hands on it. 'Any news of a house?' I asked, tentatively.

'Yes,' was the unexpected answer. 'But I don't think you will want to pay the rent. It's a beautiful house, right on the beach in a secluded area, fully furnished. But the owner's asking £360 a month.'

'I could afford it,' I said, 'but you are quite right, I don't want to pay that much money. And there's nothing else?'

He studied us for a while. 'There is another place – but I don't want to insult you.'

'Try us,' I said. 'We're pretty thick-skinned.'

'I have to contact someone,' he replied, hesitantly. 'Could I ask you please to come back at five o'clock? I've just heard that I must go to Cali the day after tomorrow for a conference, and I must find the missing five million.' Again he hesitated. 'It isn't exactly a palace, what I have in mind, but it is right on the shore and just outside Tumaco where you could build your boat in peace.'

'Look,' I assured him, 'if it has a roof and we can build our boat there, that's all we want. How much is it?'

'Oh, I don't think you would have to pay any rent,' he said, chuckling. 'By the way, I drew 10,000 pesos from my bank this morning for you. That should keep the wolf from the door. I'll see you at five?'

Thanking him profusely, we said yes and left.

Trudging back along the hot, dusty, unpaved road – with Rory complaining that his one and only pair of boots was crippling him – Redmond commented: 'I don't understand it, Dad. Why does everyone believe you and act nice to us?'

'Yes,' said Yeannie, 'it is incredible. First Señora de Lopez lent us 1,000 pesos, the major and the captain were instantly helpful, and Panchano is willing to buy wood for us.'

85

'And now,' Rory joined in. 'Jerry has lent four perfect strangers almost £70. I doubt if I would lend £70 to a friend.'

'It's because of my blue eyes and terrific personality,' I said, gaily. To which I received the expected reply of 'Bollocks!' 'No,' I went on, seriously, 'I don't know why, either. It's very strange.'

'Perhaps,' suggested Redmond, 'our story and predicament are so absurd, they've got to be true.'

'You may have hit the nail . . .' A horrible squeal and a woman's screech halted me, and almost caused us all to leap into the air with fright. We turned, and there, galloping towards us, was a small black pig with the handle of a knife sticking from its throat, blood spurting to the side, and a near-hysterical woman and three screaming kids running after it.

When the pig was only a few yards from us, it slowed, stopped, lay down and died – turning the woman's and kids' hullabaloo to shouts of victory.

'Another of the many charming facets of Tumaco,' I observed.

'Obviously, the bitch didn't have the knack,' commented Rory, smugly. 'Now *I* could have killed it instantly.'

'Big head,' said Redmond.

'Returning to what we were saying before the interruption,' I said, '. . . I wonder if she knows how to skin and gut it . . . ?'

'She'll probably cook it whole and eat it, guts, shit and all,' said Rory.

'As we were saying,' I continued, 'I think I owe it to Jerry to prove that I am an author and that I do have money. I don't know why, but I just want to. So I'll take him all my newspaper cuttings at five o'clock.'

'It would be better if you could take him your book,' snorted Redmond.

'It wasn't my bloody fault that it sold out in the first week,' I retorted, 'and that my six free copies went like hot cakes.'

86

8

Only Yeannie and I went back at five o'clock, the boys once more electing to stay in the cool of the hotel. I didn't mind because with just the two of us we weren't stared at so much.

Jerry was just putting down the phone as we were shown into his office. 'That was the owner of the house,' he said. 'It's yours if you want it – and there's no rent to pay.'

'Fantastic,' I said. 'We're very grateful for what you're doing for us.'

'See the house first before you thank me,' Jerry rejoined. 'I must warn you that there's no furniture and it will want doing up a bit; but I can help you with materials.'

'Anything will be better than what the hotel is costing,' said Yeannie.

'OK. If you want to see it I can arrange for a jeep to take you right now. The house isn't all that far. It's on this road about a kilometre past the small mainland bridge. You would have passed it when you came in on the bus.'

'Of course we want to see it,' I said. 'By the way, have you found the missing five million pesos?'

'Oh, yes,' he replied, pulling a face. 'One of my secretaries – so-called – hadn't given me all the petrol accounts, although she swore that she had. I have to put up with that sort of thing all the time.'

I handed him a large, brown envelope, containing newspaper and magazine articles about me and my book. 'What's this?' he asked, opening it. I told him and added: 'I just wanted you to know that despite what it may look like in our present circumstances we are not really bums and that you'll get your 10,000 back.'

He shook his head, highly amused. 'I never for one

moment thought you were,' he said, glancing at the envelope's contents. 'Thanks, just the same. These look pretty interesting. Can I keep them and read them later?' I nodded. 'All right,' he continued, 'let me arrange for your jeep. I'll be working here until seven this evening, so come back and let me know the verdict.'

The small mainland bridge was obviously a meeting place for men to sit, chat and watch the dug-out canoes pass under it. As our driver tooted his way through them, we saw a large cargo boat lying off Tumaco's shore, its bow in the sand and its stern in the water.

'What's that boat?' I asked.

The driver grinned. 'That was a present to the people of Tumaco from the wife of Colombia's president. It went aground and no one is interested in it. It's been there for quite a long time.'

'The president is not liked very much here, then?' commented Yeannie.

A broader grin from the driver. 'I think you could say that.'

'It will be nice to be away from all those buildings and people,' said Yeannie. 'Look, Gerald, it's all open space on the left.' On the right were the timber yards, lining the water's edge. We passed by two small stores then turned right down a small drive through clusters of giant bamboo taller than the nearby coconut palms. At the end of the drive, to the right and by the sea, was a mansion of a place, standing on nine-foot stilts and in immaculate condition.

'I don't suppose that's ours,' sighed Yeannie.

The driver laughed. 'No,' he said, starting to turn the wheel to the left round the corner of shoulder-high grass. 'This is your house.' In a way, it was like going past a Rolls Royce in the car park and getting into a clapped-out Ford. Nonetheless, Yeannie squeezed my hand with excitement.

Our 'house' was a very big, black-wood bungalow with a long verandah. Completely enclosing its accompanying expanse of land was a nine-foot-high fence of upright, pointed planks like palisades, giving a fortress-like appearance. 'Hey, this is pretty good,' I exclaimed.

'Wonderful,' said Yeannie. 'The sea is only ten metres away.'

The front and back doors were locked and all the windows were shuttered; but we estimated, correctly, that there were six rooms plus toilet and shower. So far as I could see, there were no holes in the rusty corrugated iron roof.

'Well, my darling,' I said, 'it looks like we have found our place to build our boat. Happy?'

'Oh, yes,' she said, fervently. 'Very. We'll make it a really beautiful house. Jerry is a marvellous person.'

On the other side of the house from the 'mansion' there seemed to be nothing but the tall grass, bananas and palms. Dusk was descending, and as we were about to leave, a voice called to us from the 'mansion'. On the high verandah stood a tall middle-aged woman. We walked the thirty yards or so over to her. 'Hola!' she said, again. 'Are you going to be our neighbours?'

'Yes,' said Yeannie.

'Then please come in for a minute.'

Yeannie and I walked up the long wooden stairs which were covered with a non-slip material. Close to, I could see that she was quite handsome and, judging by her high cheekbones, a beauty in her day. She introduced herself as Mercedes Benitez. She opened first a fly-screen door then the main door. The room that we entered was magnificent. Polished floor like a ballroom's. Walls and high ceiling of expensive timber. And the whole was tastefully and comfortably furnished. Not a cobweb or speck of dust to be seen.

Rising from a plush sofa, a distinguished-looking man also welcomed us. 'I am Hugo, Mercedes' husband,' he said. 'Would you like a drink? Whisky? Rum?' Yeannie and I both asked for the latter.

When we were settled with our drinks, Mercedes said: 'Tell us about yourselves. And what brought you to Tumaco?' Once more, Yeannie went into the saga, but shortened this time.

Mercedes clapped her hands at the end of it. 'Absolutely fascinating,' she said. 'We can help you with your boat – we have lots of tools. And Alex, our son, who is in the jungle at the moment, will be thrilled! Anything you want, you must ask. It will be nice to have good neighbours instead of the horrid negro who lives in the house on the other side of yours.'

'There's another house here?' I queried. 'We never saw it.'

'No, the grass is very high,' said Hugo. 'The house is about fifty or seventy-five metres from you. The negro is a very bad man and he is a little crazy. He shoots at everyone with his shotgun. Sometimes he shoots at this house, and Alex shoots back.'

'Sometimes, guns are going off at night,' Mercedes added. 'He is bad, bad, bad. One night he cut the water pipe from this house to yours – we will repair it tomorrow so you will have water – and always he is saying that all the land that your house stands on is his.'

Lovely, I thought. Good old Jerry. Plonking us smack, bang between two fightin', feudin' neighbours. No wonder he was a little abashed.

'How long has our house been empty?' I asked.

'About eighteen months,' said Hugo. 'I think it was owned by Plan de Padrinos, then a fisherman bought it. The last person to live there was a Canadian. He was always drunk, and black prostitutes were always visiting the house.'

At that moment a beautiful girl of Yeannie's age entered the room. 'This is Sonia,' said Mercedes. Sonia poured herself a whisky and sat, staring at me without comment for the rest of the conversation. Yeannie and I assumed that she was their daughter. I thought that Sonia would go down well with my sons.

'Will you be frightened to live there with the crazy negro next to you?' Mercedes asked.

'No,' I said. 'I have two big sons who know how to look after themselves, and we have a rifle.' I didn't say that it was an air rifle. But many people under-estimate an air

90

rifle, especially a .22 Airsporter. At forty yards it will put a pellet through a rabbit's head, and, as the Peruvian frontier police had rightly surmised, it could kill a man through the eye or the throat.

'Good,' said Mercedes. 'You shoot him if there is any trouble. No one will complain.'

'Why are there so many negroes in Tumaco?' Yeannie asked.

'The Americans brought them here when we had oil,' said Hugo. 'The Americans also started many other commercial enterprises. This was a big port then. But our government demanded very high taxes and, I am sorry to say, my people also robbed the Americans whenever they could. So the Americans left, the port died and we Colombians were left with a big and unwanted negro problem.'

'Trust the Yanks to do something like that,' I said. 'They cause chaos wherever they go.'

Yeannie and I got back to Jerry's office at six thirty, and told him that we thought the house was really good.

'We met the Benitez family,' said Yeannie. 'They invited us in for drinks. I like them very much.'

'But,' I added, 'you didn't tell us about the trigger-happy neighbour on the other side.'

'Didn't I?' Jerry's face was angelic innocence. 'Well, if there is any trouble, let me know.'

'Yeah,' I said. 'We'll crawl, bleeding, to your medical department to take out the buckshot. Seriously, though, we think the house is ideal. When can we move in?'

'Tomorrow if you like. The same driver can meet you at your hotel at ten in the morning, and take you shopping for food and things. He'll show you the right shops so that you pay the right prices. And he'll get the key from the owner. I should be over to see you about five when I've finished all my paper work, so if you'll make a list of things you want to make the house more comfortable – wood, paint, nails, etc – I can arrange for those things. And I would appreciate it if you could give the driver 500 pesos for his trouble.'

Señora de Lopez and the boys – especially the boys –

91

were very pleased when we told them the news. I explained to the señora that it might be two weeks or more before my money arrived. 'No problem,' she said, 'but could you please pay for your drinks? I have to settle that account every week.' So I paid her and returned the 1,000 pesos she had lent us. Also, as a gesture, I left my typewriter as security.

Next morning, with much excitement because we now had a house of our own in an isolated spot, we loaded up the jeep and went on a shopping spree: potatoes, flour, rice, onions, spices, tea, coffee, sugar, powdered milk, spaghetti, tins of fish, cooking oil, fruit, margarine, tomatoes, cabbage, garlic, candles, matches and a bottle of rum. To balance out the fact that Yeannie and Redmond didn't smoke I bought a large box of chocolates which cost the same as a carton of cigarettes.

After we had deposited everything on the verandah, the driver left, very happy with his 500 pesos. Rory unlocked the front door. It was dank and dingy inside, and the walls and floors were filthy. Redmond pressed down an electric light switch and we had light – but only in the one room, for as we explored we discovered that there was only one light bulb! But the house was wired for electricity, and that was certainly a bonus. As we went from room to room we opened the shutters, revealing large rooms with high ceilings, albeit begrimed and cobwebby.

As we entered the last room, Yeannie suddenly screamed as bats zoomed past our heads, through the house and out of the front door. 'This house is bloody good,' declared Redmond.

'With paint it will be fantastic,' said Yeannie. 'I say we paint all the walls and ceilings white.' We all agreed.

We each chose a bedroom, the largest room going to Yeannie and me. The kitchen area had a concrete floor and was the filthiest part of the entire house. The actual fireplace was outside under a large awning of wood and tin and lying on its side, broken. The lavatory stank and the shower house was full of creepy-crawlies. All in all it was quite reasonable after standing empty for eighteen months. And the whole area smacked of tranquillity. Budgerigars fluttered outside with humming birds and other birds of bright colours. In the trunk of a dead coconut palm a woodpecker had nested. Many beautiful wild flowers grew all round and in the somewhat cluttered and overgrown garden.

'I want to do the garden,' enthused Yeannie, 'and put flowers all over the house.'

'Better let Rory and Redmond clear it a bit first with machetes,' I said. 'There's probably quite a few snakes in there. Where are you going to put the coffee plant?'

'In our bedroom, of course. It needs love and talking to.'

'I think water will be sufficient,' I replied, laughing.

Mercedes came round to be introduced to the boys. 'My! They are handsome!' she whispered to me. 'Good strong shoulders, too.' She asked if she could borrow the boys to help fix the water-pipe.

Alex Benitez was our next visitor. He had blue, devil-may-care eyes and sported a black beard tinged with red. When he smiled, he looked quite swashbuckling. He confirmed what I had thought about there being snakes there. One that he described sounded to me like a coral snake. 'But there is a more deadly one,' he said. 'It is light and dark brown and we call it simply "X", the letter of the alphabet.' He pronounced the X as ekkiss. 'Only a few weeks ago I shot one on this verandah. Always have a good look round before stepping outside in the morning.' I promptly named the snake the 'Kiss of death'.

Alex stayed with us talking for quite a while. 'Now I must see to my fighting cocks,' he said. 'Tonight there is a big fight and I'm hoping to win a lot of money. I think my father and mother are preparing you a welcome meal for this evening.'

All afternoon we were sweeping, washing and cleaning the house. 'It's like Pususquere all over again,' said Rory, 'except that this time we'll have a decent house when we've finished.'

It was delicious, too, to be able to dive into the sea

93

when our bodies became dirt-streaked with sweat. We were on the shore of a lagoon formed by the mainland, Tumaco and a long, narrow, uninhabited island with many palms. On the other side of the island we could see the Pacific broiling white and shooting the spume high into the air. 'It does look a bit rough out there, Dad,' commented Redmond. 'I expect I'll spew until I get to the calm.' Sea-sickness was always a problem with him. 'I'm going to write to grandma and ask her to send me some Kwells.'

Our first evening and night in the house were quite eventful. Jerry arrived on his motorcycle and took a list of all the things we needed. I immediately poured him a tumbler of rum. 'Who was the Canadian who lived here?' I asked. 'A friend of yours?'

'Not really. He arrived here more destitute than you people are. The Colombians have a very subtle way of robbing people. They offer you a piece of chocolate that is doped. Never take a piece of chocolate from anybody here. He was on the bus alone, travelling down from Pasto, the capital of Narino, and he took a piece of chocolate. When he woke up in Tumaco, his wallet, pass-port, everything was gone. I gave him some money and he did some work for Plan. But he drank a lot. In the end I paid his air fare to Bogotá so he could contact the Canadian Embassy and get home.'

'You're quite the Samaritan,' I said. 'How long will you be away in Cali?'

'About a week. You should be quite established here when I get back. The driver will be here early tomorrow morning with all the things you need. I think this house has a lot of potential.'

Just after dark, Hugo and Mercedes arrived with a large basket of roast chicken and chips and a bottle of Aguardiente, the commercialised equivalent of *anisado*.

'We drink!' said Hugo, with the resolute air of a man who likes his liquor. We sat on the now clean floor under our one and only lamp bulb and had quite an enjoyable meal with good conversation. That is, until the light went out.

94

'Every night it is the same,' said Mercedes. 'The water, too. We have terrible problems with electricity and water. Some evenings when the lights go out we forget to turn off the switches. Then, about two o'clock in the morning, the electricity comes back on and wakes us all up. Try your water. I bet it's off.' It was, too. 'That will also come back on in the night.'

We learnt that Hugo was a financial adviser to the government and that Sonia was Alex's wife. They had a little boy called Alexandro.

When they'd gone, we all, strangely enough, felt hungry. 'I want some more chips,' said Rory. We thought that an excellent idea. There was plenty of water in the saucepan too, for coffee. We lit a fire on the concrete, kitchen floor because we hadn't the nails to mend the fireplace. When we went to bed with our bellies full, the fire was still burning. 'It will keep the flies and mosquitoes out,' I said.

We hadn't been in bed half an hour when, from somewhere across the tall grass, came the double blast of a shotgun and a woman's horrible scream.

A deathly silence, then a man's yell and three more shotgun blasts from a different direction. 'Did you lock the doors, Dad?' asked Rory, anxiously.

'Yes,' I said. 'Who's got the air rifle?'

'I have,' he replied. 'It's loaded and I'm keeping it!'

In a loud voice for humorous effect, I growled: 'Stop shaking, Yeannie!'

'I bet the little fart has shit herself,' said Redmond, laughing.

'No I haven't, Redmond,' she said. 'And it's your father who is shaking.' What the boys didn't appreciate was that Yeannie and I had been making love. No matter what or who else the shotguns had killed, they had certainly destroyed orgasms!

A little after ten past three in the morning, according to Redmond's watch, Yeannie woke me, urgently. 'I smell burning!' she cried.

The smell was almost overpowering. I got up immediately, shouting to the boys. Smoke was pouring from the

95

kitchen in the light of the electric bulb which had come on again. The heat from the fire had gone through the concrete and all the supporting, dry and almost rotten timbers were glowing red. Luckily, Yeannie had filled the two outside washtubs with water in which clothes were soaking. With saucepans and buckets we soon emptied those. It took nearly an hour to put all the wood out, and we had to smash the concrete floor with the back of the axe to get at the beams right underneath.

'I think we'll have to build a new kitchen floor tomorrow, Dad,' said Redmond.

'Fancy building a concrete floor on top of wooden supports,' was Rory's disgusted comment.

Above left: sailing to the Galapagos Islands. Yeannie with the captain of the *Buccaneer*, Señor Danilo.

Above right: the *Buccaneer* dwarfed by Darwin's Lagoon on Isabela Island.

Below: seals enjoying themselves on Fernandina Island.

Above: Alex and Sonia outside their beach hut.

Below: some of Tumaco's youth. The man on the left worked for Alex.

Above: Redmond and Rory going up jungle in Arthur's canoe.

Below: outside Maximino's house, cacao beans in the foreground.

Above: Rory and Alex make the first cuts in the ceibo tree's trunk and vanes.

Below: the author, with bandaged hand, continues work on the trunk.

Jeannie gives an idea of the trunk's diameter while work progresses on the canoe.

Above: preparing to move the canoe through the jungle to the coast. Onofre (centre) is in the red cap.

Below: the canoe on the move.

Above: Redmond and Rory smooth the underside of the canoe.
Below: fixing metal bands for extra strength.

Above: ready for the off. In the foreground is Arthur's canoe which was used to take supplies out to the boat.

Below: Yeannie, after the adventure, on the ranch in the Chilean Andes.

9

It was ten days before Jerry came to see us again. He couldn't believe the change in the house. Outside the verandah, the grass and weeds had been cleared, the three young coconut palms had been pruned and there were borders of wild flowers. Transplantation presents no difficulties in the tropics.

The inside of the house was a blaze of white. Because we had sufficient paint, Yeannie and I had painted our bedroom floor white as well! We had ripped away the outside kitchen wall and used the timber to rebuild the kitchen floor and replace the floor joists. It was now white, airy, open-plan. The fireplace was truly a work of art, and the lavatory bowl was spotless. We had built beds, a kitchen table and bench seats. There were even shelves, working surfaces and wardrobes.

'My goodness,' he said, 'you have been busy.' I gave him a tumbler of rum, for I could sense that he was troubled. He took a big swig. 'I have a big problem,' he sighed. 'DAS have told me their Intelligence Department has caught wind of a group of people wanting to kidnap me.'

'What?' I exclaimed, for it was the only answer I could think of.

He nodded, solemnly. 'I have to carry this.' He opened his leather handbag, which all Colombians use, and produced a snub-nosed .38 automatic. 'Isn't it incredible?' he said. 'I have sent my son to his mother's for safety.'

'I know it's a daft thing to say in my circumstances, but if there's anything I can do to help . . .'

'No,' he said, emptying the glass. 'DAS are very efficient.'

'I sincerely hope so,' I said. 'It must be bloody awful having that hanging over your head.'

'How have things been with you?' he asked.

'Pretty good. Night-times are a bit scary with all the shotguns going off and people shouting. One night, Alex let loose with his .38. It sounds like a bloody cannon in the dead of night. What *do* they shoot at? No one ever seems to get hit.'

'I think they fire mostly into the air,' he said. 'Speaking of .38s, I need some practice, and this is a good enough spot. By the way, where are the others?'

'Either on our raft – or, if I know them, swimming with Alex and family.'

We went out and down to the beach. Sure enough, there they all were, splashing, swimming and laughing.

'Where's all the fish?' I called. 'And look, we have a visitor!' They all came out of the sea. Hugo went to the mansion and fetched a bottle of Johnnie Walker.

'Is that your raft?' asked Jerry, when all the welcomes were over.

'Yes,' I said, 'it seats four of us – arses in the water, of course – and it's nothing but bamboo and rope, a trick I learned on Cocos Island where the surf was so tremendous it would just tear out nails.'

The Benitezes, Yeannie and the boys were shocked when I told them about the kidnap threat to Jerry. 'DAS will get them,' Hugo said, confidently. 'Come,' he commanded, 'let us drink.'

But Jerry, Alex and the boys opted out after a few sips and began blasting away with the .38 at a tin can they had thrown into the sea.

'Hey,' I called, 'it's Jerry who needs the practice, not you lot.' So Alex fetched his .38. Thankfully, the whisky helped to muffle the detonations.

'When will you start to build your boat?' Hugo asked. 'I am very interested in the project. And Alex must go with you to buy the wood. He knows the right people.'

'Just as soon as my money arrives. About another week now.'

'It is strange that you want to build a boat and sail to England,' observed Mercedes, 'for you never care much to swim.'

'Ah,' I said, 'that is because when I was in Malaya in the Army I did a lot of high diving into very deep water, and my sinuses were affected. Any water going up my nose, or pressure on my ears, gives me a lot of pain. But I really like the sea. I don't think I have ever been afraid of it on a boat.'

That evening when we were eating dinner, Yeannie said: 'I feel very sad about Jerry. He's such a nice man and, as Hugo told us, he and Plan de Padrinos have done a lot for the negroes here. It must be terrible, knowing that someone wants to kidnap you.'

'That's one thing we'll never have to worry about,' commented Redmond. 'Being kidnapped.'

'Yeah,' said Rory, 'we've no money!'

Almost a week later Arthur, the American, came to see us. He was tall and lean and had a thick but well-trimmed sandy beard. The bank wanted to see Rory about his cheque. Arthur accepted coffee and he told us he had turned his back on the United States because of the politics and 'false economy'. He never wanted to go back. He liked Tumaco and he had married a negress. They had a small child.

'Any news about Jerry's situation?' I asked.

'Yes. DAS now know who the men are, so it shouldn't be long before they get them.'

Arthur took Rory on the back of his motorcycle to the bank. 'If the money's there, I'll buy a few things and a bottle of brandy to celebrate,' he said. But he returned empty-handed, hot, angry and totally fed up. 'The bloody cheque has bounced,' he said. 'Now what are we going to do?'

'Keep calm,' I told him. 'Obviously, my cheque never got to your bank in time. I'm going in to see Jerry.' Yeannie went with us. The first thing Jerry asked was at which post office had I handed in the letter.

'The one by the bank, of course,' I said, rather perplexed. 'We've sent all our mail from there.'

'That's only for local mail,' he said. 'There's another one for airmail. How much postage did you pay?' I told him. 'Your letter's probably gone by sea. It costs 115 pesos to send a letter to Canada!'

The only thing he could suggest was that I gave him a cheque for £1,000 and he would pay it into his account. 'But that will take three weeks just the same,' he added.

'Three more weeks before we can start buying timber,' I groaned as I wrote the cheque, 'and what are we going to do about food?'

'I can let you have another 6,000 pesos. But that's all, I'm afraid. Plan isn't like other charitable organisations – the people get the money, not the directors! You'll have to re-think your situation. There isn't time now for Panchano to build your boat and none of these timber merchants give credit.'

'What chance is there of getting DAS to give us more time?'

'Very slim,' said Jerry. 'Governments here treat people from other parts of the world the same way as their own people are treated in certain other countries. For instance, can you imagine what your English authorities would say if four Colombians arrived there with no money, and saying they wanted to build a boat and sail back to Colombia? They'd kick their arses on to the first available plane. So why should Colombia behave any different to you just because you are English? You could, probably, get more time if you were willing to pay. But with four of you that could mean a lot of money.'

'I take your point,' I said. 'It's the same old story about money knowing no frontiers – that's what makes the whole passport system farcical in my opinion. And passports have never stopped the unwanted from getting into England – or into any other country for that matter.'

On the walk back to the house, I made up my mind what I was going to do. Alex was at the front of his house with several of his cockerels tethered by one leg to wooden stakes in the ground. He was teaching a young one to fight by waving a pecking, clawing older bird in front of its head. I told him our latest news and asked how much a tree-trunk would cost.

'About 20,000 pesos. Do you intend to go to England in a dug-out canoe?'

'I don't see there is any alternative,' I said. 'And a trunk would certainly save time because we wouldn't have to build a keel. Just add sides above it.'

'I could get you a tree-trunk for nothing,' he said. 'There are many big trees in that part of the jungle I am overseeing, and they will all be cut down when the area is cleared to make a shrimp farm. I promised Rory I would take him tomorrow. We can see what trees there are.'

'I want the largest and widest trunk possible,' I told him. 'I don't fancy doing what these people do to make their canoes wider, the joins always leak and it wouldn't be very nice if the inserted section fell out halfway to England!'

'Then I think you will need a ceibo tree. They are of the balsa family, but harder wood and very big trunks. I will ask Maximino tomorrow. He works for me and he lives in the jungle.'

'Do many people live in the jungle here?'

Alex nodded. 'There are three tribes of negroes – and there is always trouble. They live by the law of the machete. In the last year there have been sixteen murders! There are always robberies and fighting between the different families.'

'And Maximino? Is he Colombian?'

'No, negro. But he is not a member of one of the tribes and he lives with his family away from the villages. He is a very good man and my friend.'

'Well, look out for Rory, tomorrow,' I said.

'Yes. I always take my .38 with me. But I am only going to see Maximino, then I will visit my grandfather. He has a big farm in another part of the jungle.'

At five o'clock the next afternoon I went down to the beach to watch for Alex's aluminium dinghy, which had a 25 hp outboard. Alex had told me they would be back about half past four. I was just beginning to fret when I saw the boat come shooting out from under the mainland bridge. As it came speeding towards me, I could see Rory and Alex laughing.

'Hiya, Dad!' Rory called. 'Guess who's drunk?'

They both were. 'Fantastic day!' he said, as he threw the anchor rope to me. 'I've been horse-riding! I still remembered from the days in Italy.'

'Good,' I said, as I pulled them ashore. 'But what about a tree?'

'Good news,' he said, laughing and almost falling out of the boat clutching a big bunch of bananas. 'These are for us – and we've got oranges, too. God, I could do with a drink of coffee.'

'Three ceibos,' Alex told me, his blue eyes sparkling with alcohol. 'We have drunk a little Aguardiente.' Sonia had also come down to the beach, and she raised her eyebrows at me, laughing. 'In two days' time I will take you to see them. Very, very big.' With that, he half dived, half fell into the sea. Sonia instantly joined him, splashing him vigorously and giggling.

Rory was not only full of Aguardiente but full of the day's adventure. He prattled on about it while Yeannie made coffee.

'The reason Alex can take only one person at a time this week is because he loads the boat up in Tumaco with materials for Maximino's new house. I like Maximino. He is different from the town people. In fact, they all are up there. Maximino lives in a shack with a grass roof at the end of a long, narrow creek which is knee-deep with mud when the tide goes out.

'But, Dad, the jungle is beautiful and there's land for sale next to the waterways. I wouldn't mind living there. But there are lots of snakes. From where we left the dinghy to his grandfather's farm is bloody miles. Alex always lets one of the locals walk in front because they can smell the snakes. We came to two trees, growing close together and, if I'd been on my own I would have walked between them. But the man in front said no, there was an ekkiss there, waiting. He cut out a big turf with his machete and threw

102

it between the trees. There was a sort of blurred movement and the snake went off like the clappers. The ekkiss is ever so big, Dad. About six feet. All its back is dark brown, and its belly is like milky coffee. Apparently, they always lie in wait near paths. I wouldn't like to go walking about there on my own.'

'Where did you start drinking?' I asked. 'At Alex's grandfather's?'

'We just had a couple of glasses there with a huge meal – a giant beef steak, about two inches thick. No, we went back to the village where we had left the dinghy but the tide was out, so we went to one of the huts where several of the villagers that Alex sometimes employs were drinking. I reckon we put away about four bottles of Aguardiente.

'They are a pretty wild-looking bunch, but very friendly. One thing I noticed, not one of them goes anywhere without his machete. Even while they were drinking, two of them just sat there, sharpening their machetes on big, flat stones. The machetes are like another hand. As Alex said, the machete definitely rules in the villages. And they are razor sharp.

'And another thing I found out. You know we've seen crippled negroes in Tumaco? Remember one we saw without hands? That's because of dynamite. They use it for fishing. But sometimes one of the charges hasn't exploded before they dive into the water for the fish, and away goes a hand, foot or even a leg.'

'How long does it take to get to where the ceibos are?' I asked.

'More than an hour in the dinghy. It's well over ten miles, Dad. Then we'll have the problem of getting the trunk to Maximino's house where the nearest water is, and that's quite a way. It's going to be a lot of hard work. Alex reckons it will take three days to chop the tree down. It's a helluva size. Wait till you see it. The other two ceibos aren't quite so thick. But all their trunks are dead straight.'

Yeannie placed a mug of coffee in front of him. 'Thanks,' he said. 'One more thing, Dad. One of the men told me that ceibo only lasts for six months in the sea.

103

That's why they never use it for dug-outs. After six months, it splits.'

'But we've calculated it will take only three months to get to England,' I pointed out. 'And only one or two people here use paint on their dug-outs. What does Alex think? And what do you three think? You were both against building a dug-out when I suggested it yesterday.'

'Alex seems to think it's the best idea in view of the time factor.'

'And I'll go along with that,' said Redmond. 'Knocking a bloody big tree down quite appeals. And try to get it right this time, Dad. Remember in Italy? The big tree we felled? You swore blind that it would miss the power cables. And we put all the lights out in Monte Quiesa!'

Rory began laughing. 'And what about in Rowden Paddocks? Pete said whatever you do I don't want the tree to fall on the hedge. And it squashed yards of the hedge as flat as a pancake!'

'Yes, well, anyone can make a mistake,' I said.

'You know,' said Redmond, 'I feel quite excited now that we've got a tree. I think it's actually going to happen that we sail to England.'

'And you, Yeannie?' I asked. 'You're very quiet.'

'It is possibly a good idea for adventure, but I think it needs more elaboration – more time. It could be that you are simply looking for danger. Perhaps that is your life. I like an adventure when it has a purpose, a meaning. And the sea always fills me with panic. But I will go.'

'This has a meaning,' said Redmond, laughing. 'It means we get to England cheap!'

'What have you lot been doing all day?' Rory wanted to know.

'For the most part of it,' I said, 'writing letters to go from the correct post office. Then we tried a bit of fishing from the raft. Sod all fish, as usual. Then, also as usual, the raft has been used as a diving stage by Redmond, Sonia, the two coloured servants and a load of little urchins. God knows where they all come from. And, I don't want to grass, but who tried pinching the bum of the coloured girl?'

'Redmond,' declared Yeannie, laughing.

'Dirty, filthy beast,' said Rory, with mock disgust. 'I'm going to bed.'

10

Without the presence of monkeys, the jungle is a deathly quiet place, the thick foliage dampening and occluding many sounds from the area a person is in. Yet, paradoxically, there is always some noise: a large leaf falling to the ground, or fruit falling, a rustle in the undergrowth, the call of a bird, a tree creaking, the buzz of insects, something unseen hurrying away.

But those sounds always exaggerate, not obliterate, the jungle's aura of silence.

In the Cocos Island jungle, a rifle could be fired and not heard 250 metres away. When there are monkeys overhead there is no silence – only incessant cacophony. But fire a rifle and the monkeys' chattering stops immediately and the silence can actually smite one's ears. After a moment or two, the bravest monkey will put out an investigative call. Another will answer, then another and another until the chorus is once more in full swing.

The Colombian jungle had no monkeys in the part where Maximino and I were walking, even though it was rich with bananas, cacao, oranges and other fruit. 'The monkeys live many, many kilometres inland,' he told me.

Maximino was leading the way to the largest ceibo. In his right hand he carried a machete. His left hand held the single barrel of a 16-bore shotgun slung over his left shoulder. Maximino was in his mid-sixties and his black, wrinkled face seemed always to be wreathed with humour. He also had a nasty habit of stopping and turning to point something out to me, for each time I found myself looking down the muzzle of his gun. 'You're pointing your gun at me again,' I would exclaim, and he would casually avert the barrel so that if the gun did go off accidentally – it was quite ancient and the safety catch was broken – the shot would miss me by at least a yard! And he'd carry on talking, quite unconcernedly. Almost the first thing Alex had said to him after introducing me was: 'For God's sake, Maximino, the gun's pointing straight at my head!' But Maximino had always carried a gun like that, and he was too old to change.

Alex had left me in Maximino's tender care to go further up the waterway to the village to talk business. 'When you've seen the tree, Maximino will give you lunch and bring you to the village,' he'd said. I was quite happy. I was going to see *my* tree, and Maximino had that quiet air of assurance of a man who knows exactly what he's doing.

One of the more interesting things he pointed out to me was a rat trap. Quite a simple and extremely lethal affair. A rectangle of upright sticks close together, like the fence of our house but in miniature, with an opening for the rat to enter to take the crab bait. As the rat took it, pressure was released on two fulcrums and down came two very heavy logs, one on top of the other to fit with a clunk exactly inside the barricade. 'God,' I said, 'the rat must be squashed flat!'

'Yes,' said Maximino, 'but the important thing is it is dead! And it is very good food. We eat a lot of rat.'

There seemed to be land crabs everywhere, some of them quite large. They were bright red and creamy-beige and were easy to see against the green. 'These, too, are excellent for eating,' said Maximino. I felt I could agree with him about the crabs.

Just after we had left the main trail for one that was scanty and overgrown, we came to a large bush on one side and a tree on the other. Maximino raised his machete for me to halt. Then he stuck it into the ground and stepped carefully forward with the shotgun at the ready in both hands. Suddenly he brought the butt to his shoulder and fired. I could see the high loops the snake made in its death throes. It had obviously been lying coiled ready to strike because the buckshot had ripped numerous gashes in its body, as well as just behind the head. 'Ekkiss,' said Maximino.

Telling me to keep a careful watch he cleared a large area with his machete all round the wriggling and twitching snake. The boys and Alex saw the place later and they, too, estimated that Maximino had cleared a 15-foot diameter circle with the trail running between. He also hacked down the bush. Next, he dug a fairly deep hole with his machete. Then he did something I have seen done in several countries but still don't know if there is any truth in the reason for it. He cut off the snake's head and smashed the eyes to smithereens. The belief is that a snake will photograph with its eyes the thing that kills it, and its mate will see that image in the dead eyes and track down the killer.

When I was a little boy, I saw my father do the same thing with an adder. In Italy a workman, with the usual volatile excitability of his race, smashed the head of a grass snake even though I insisted it wasn't a viper! In Australia, Malaya and China I have seen the same thing. So is there any truth in it? I don't know. I'm inclined to think that the story is as mythical as the one claiming that a snake never dies until the sun goes down.

Maximino put the head and body into the hole and filled it in. Finally, he cut a sapling, stripped off the bark and stuck it into the mound. This, he told me, was the sign to other people that an ekkiss was buried there and to be on guard for its mate.

We carried on walking and came to the tree very suddenly and quite unexpectedly. Maximino had turned sharply left through some bananas, and there was the ceibo – a veritable giant of a tree. I had to tilt my head back to look up its high, wide and straight trunk to where its first branches started way beyond the other trees. I felt quite in awe of it.

'What do you think its diameter is?' I asked.

'About one and a quarter metres,' said Maximino. 'It will make a giant canoe.'

The tree's immensity and thick, long branches were held firm by a central root and six others that started about eight feet up the trunk and extended downwards in enormous vanes like the tail fins of a giant rocket. Each was about eighteen inches thick and the bases some ten feet wide.

'How many axes do you have?' I asked.

'Two,' he said.

'May we borrow them?'

'Of course. When will you start? It won't be easy cutting it down. A lot of work.'

'Next week,' I said, 'when Alex can bring me and my two sons here.'

'I would appreciate it very much,' said Maximino, walking into the banana grove, 'if you could make the tree fall this way because on the other side are many cacaos and I sell the fruit to make chocolate.'

'I understand,' I said. 'I'll do what I can.'

While Maximino cleared a path all round the massive trunk, I stood looking at the tree, calculating how long it would take to fell it. To cut through each vane would take at least an hour. With three of us swinging axes that would mean two hours. Another two hours to cut the deep vee so that it would fall the right way, then another three hours to topple it. Allowing another hour for eating and resting would mean a total of eight hours. So if we started at ten in the morning, the tree, hopefully, would be on the ground about six in the evening.

As I stood there, looking at the tree, I felt quite insignificant against its size and majesty. A pang of extreme sorrow ran through me. What right had I to kill it? It represented years and years of living and steadfast growth. And now some foreign Englishman was going to cut it down because of a stupid idea of making it into a boat and sailing it to England.

'Would you like to go to England?' I asked it in English, like a complete moron. And, of course, there was no answer. 'You are going to be the biggest dug-out Tumaco has ever seen. Isn't that something to be proud of? Much better than standing in this nasty old snake-infested jungle. You are going to *be* something.'

The swishing machete appeared round the corner of one

109

of the huge vanes, Maximino's sweating face behind it. 'What did you say?' he asked.

'I was talking to the tree,' I told him.

'Ah!' His tone was of complete understanding. He didn't like killing big trees, either. 'I always think that perhaps the tree will have its revenge and fall on top of me,' he said.

I remembered a short story I had read many years before about a man who wanted to cut down a big tree. As the blade of the axe bit into the trunk with the first swing, there came a tremendous scream from above. It was getting dark and the man thought he must be hearing things because he was tired. So he decided to wait until next morning. In the cold light of dawn when the scream came again and again with the chopping of the axe, the man ignored it. An hour later when he stopped to rest, a huge branch suddenly fell from the tree and killed him.

The ceibo's branches were very big, and I felt a tinge of fear, a strong premonition that, right from the receipt of Yeannie's letter, all that had happened had occurred in order that I would be here in this jungle so that the ceibo could kill me.

Then I told myself not to be so bloody silly. I'd had hundreds of premonitions in my life and not one of them had come to anything. Perhaps the worst and longest-lasting was when I had stood on the deck of the troopship *Halladale* which was taking me to Korea, and I had watched England's shores fade behind. I was a twenty-two-year-old paratrooper, supposedly one of the fearless hairy-arses, yet I knew for certain I would never see England again. That premonition had been with me for almost the whole of the eighteen months I was there, thirteen of which were as a Forward Observation Post signaller. Yet the incessant fear within me had never shown and always Captain Legg chose me for a 'tricky situation'. There was one time, though, when even the devil-may-care Captain Legg's anal sphincter twitched. We were digging in a new position on the forward slopes in daylight. Suddenly, a sniper's bullet put a neat hole through the spade I was using, and we both leapt into the trench. We needed more sandbags but they were above in full view of 'Chinky' as the enemy was known.

'Fancy winning the VC today?' he asked.

'No. I don't think so.'

'Neither do I. Fuck it. The sandbags can stay there till nightfall.'

I wondered what Captain Legg was doing now and what he would think if he knew my feelings about this tree. Perhaps one day I would put an advertisement in *The Times*, calling for a reunion of all the men of 120 Battery of Mortars. It had been formed hurriedly as a bastard unit to replace the battery that was wiped out to the man with the 'Glorious Gloucesters'. We always reckoned that we were a bloody fine bunch of bastards!

On the way back to Maximino's shack, he made the short trail to the main one more distinct. I offered to carry his shotgun but he said no, he felt more comfortable with it on his shoulder. He was on particular guard when we passed through the clearing where the ekkiss lay. I tried to explain to him that an X in English signified a kiss and that the snake was a kiss of death. I wasn't sure if he understood, though.

Maximino's shack was two-tiered and had many holes in the aged wooden walls. His common-law wife – his real wife had gone back to Cali – was large-arsed and jovial. She had a meal of fish, rice and beans waiting for us. The kitchen-cum-eating area was on the second floor and was open-plan for there were no walls. She and Maximino's three children didn't sit at the table with us but squatted with plates on laps on the floor. This was the custom, for Women's Lib had not reached the negroes of Tumaco and its far surrounds. Come to think of it, neither had Children's Lib! I noticed, too, that everyone washed their hands in a small bowl *after* the meal, not before. This was because they adhered to the adage 'Fingers came before forks' and the only implement I was given was a spoon.

We took a different trail to the village, which was about

111

two kilometres away. It led us through a thick grove of coconut palms.

There were about seven huts in the village, all with thatched roofs. There was also a school with the words '*escuela*' daubed in white paint on the wall. I couldn't help laughing because each letter was different with a mixture of capital letters and small ones. A classic example of what a printer would call upper and lower case! A fine start to a child's education, I thought.

In one of the larger huts we found Alex and several villagers half-sprawled on the floor, with their backs against the wall, drinking Aguardiente. Immediately we entered, glasses were thrust into our hands. 'You work extremely hard, Alex,' I said, and he laughed.

'What do you think of the tree?' he wanted to know.

'Very good.' I had no chance to say more because Maximino had launched into the story of killing the ekkiss. A middle-aged woman brought in four large *pipas* – green coconuts – and cocktails were made with the cold juice and Aguardiente. I settled myself against the wall next to Alex and switched off from the Spanish conversation. Most of it was too fast and difficult to understand with the local dialect. Everyone was laughing, talking and friendly. The villagers reminded me of the Torres Strait islanders – devoid of any aggression towards an outsider. Was this because they were free, owned parcels of land and were in their natural surroundings? Their whole behaviour seemed entirely different to that of their fellows in Tumaco.

Perhaps, I thought, the world would be a far happier place if more people returned to farming – certainly there were enough wild places left that, with a pioneering spirit, could be made crop productive. Unfortunately, all races clamoured for the pseudo-security of city life – and to hell with working on the land. In France and Italy, people had been wooed from the fields to work in the car and tyre factories with near-disastrous results. In fact, I remembered the big advertisements in France in the seventies, telling the people to go back to the land for a better life. In England, too, the government has for years tried to get

112

manufacturers to move their factories north, but the bright city lights hold the bigger fascination for the gregarious populace.

Yeannie invaded my thoughts. It was the first time we had been apart for four months. Incredibly, I found I was missing her. I hoped the boys weren't teasing her too much.

'We are going to eat.' Alex's voice invaded my reverie. A tall, broad-shouldered man came in through the door. He wore only a pair of jeans and his huge chest and arm muscles glistened like polished ebony. Under one arm he had a big black chicken. Alex called to him. 'Hey, Onofre, this is the gringo who wants to build a boat.' Smiling broadly, Onofre came over and shook my hand. 'Onofre could cut down your tree in one hour!' someone boasted, and Onofre's smile grew even broader. As if to demonstrate one of his skills, he took the chicken's head in one large hand, gave a sort of dance and bow, like a stage performer, at the same time swinging the chicken's body in a wide circle as though it were weightless. Then, with another graceful bow, he placed the chicken – as dead as the proverbial dodo – on the floor. Everybody clapped, and I joined in, too. Just as the dead chicken's nerves were about to agitate its legs and wings, the woman picked it up and took it to the kitchen. Onofre plonked himself down next to me.

'Onofre makes most of the canoes for the villagers,' said Alex. 'He will hollow the trunk out for you. He has special tools and he'll make a first-class job of it.'

'How much is that going to cost me?' I asked.

'1,000 pesos a day,' replied Onofre.

I looked at Alex. He nodded. 'OK,' I said. 'It's a deal.'

'You cut the tree down, cut it to size,' said Onofre, 'and I will tell you how many days it will take. But I think no more than a maximum of ten.'

Within an hour I was feeling nicely mellow and eating a rich soup made with the chicken Onofre had killed.

'You have a weapon with you?' he asked. 'It is always best to carry a weapon in the jungle.' Again I looked at

113

Alex, and again he nodded. I took the White Hunter out of its sheath, which I'd kept hidden inside my shirt and trousers. Onofre whistled at the sight of it. I passed it to him. 'Very beautiful,' he said, balancing the long, double-edged blade and bone handle. Everybody wanted to touch it. I felt quite proud to own it. When it had gone the rounds and was back in Onofre's hands, he said: 'I will make it sharper for you.' And he fetched one of the large sharpening stones. I told him that my sons had used it on the Galapagos to cut shark, that was why it was a little blunt.

Watching Onofre sharpening it, Alex said: 'I think you should give me that knife as a memento when you leave.'

'I'll think about it,' I told him. But I knew damn well that I wouldn't.

It was Onofre who told me how, in 1974, an earthquake had changed much of the coastline around Tumaco. Before, the area had been hilly, but the quake had flattened the hills, pushing them down to the sea to make hundreds of islands, many of which, although thickly covered with vegetation, were under water at high tide. The sea now invaded the land like a river's delta.

'I know,' I said. 'When Alex turned from the sea to come up here, I thought we were actually entering the mouth of a river. And I fully expected to see crocodiles come slithering down the muddy banks.'

'We have many crocodiles in Colombia,' said Onofre, 'but they are further inland on the real, fresh-water rivers.' I told him about the sea crocodiles in the Torres Strait and he'd never heard of a crocodile living in the sea.

After explaining to him about the time factor, that we had to leave Colombia on May 9, I suggested that my sons, Yeannie and I camped by the tree each night until the canoe was ready. 'You cannot sleep in the jungle,' he said, 'or you will be dead in the morning. Not only is there the ekkiss but we also have the flying snake. They sleep in the trees in the daytime and hunt at night. They throw themselves in twos, threes or fours on to their prey. They are very lethal and a person is dead in a few minutes.'

'I heard about those in Malaya,' I said, 'but I can't remember their name. What do you people call them?'
'We just call them the snake that flies,' he said.

11

Because of the lateness of the tide, it was almost dark when Alex and I got back. The boys, Yeannie and Sonia were waiting on the beach. 'Yeannie's been sitting here since three o'clock, waiting for you!' said Redmond. 'I think she's nuts!'

At the first opportunity, Yeannie whispered: 'It's really awful but I have been very worried about you. I missed you very much.'

'Me, too,' I said. 'Anyway,' I continued, in a louder voice, 'the tree is just what we want.'

It wasn't until we were eating dinner that I told them about the flying snakes and the ekkiss that Maximino had shot.

'I'm not going up there again!' stated Rory.

'Why not? The flying snakes don't venture out in the daytime.'

'Shy, are they then, Dad?' asked Redmond, sarcastically.

'And what about if there are flying snakes in the ceibo, and the axes wake them up?' persisted Rory.

'I asked Maximino about that and he said the ceibo's branches are too high. Alex said he will take the three of us there next Tuesday or Wednesday. That's when you'll start doing some work for your living, whether you like it or not.'

'What about me?' asked Yeannie. 'I have to stay here alone?'

'You won't be alone,' I said. 'There's Mercedes and Sonia to talk to. And we'll be back before dark.'

That night, as she always did, Yeannie carefully brushed her hair and put on a sexy garment as a *pequeño sorpresa* (little surprise) for me. She always maintained that a

116

woman should look beautiful and alluring to get into bed with her man.

'What do you really think of all this? Our situation and our relationship?' I asked, as we lay side by side under the mosquito net in our vividly white bedroom.

She took her time before answering. 'What I feel for you, Gerald, often changes, but underneath I always have this strong sense of loyalty and friendship. That's not to say I don't love you!' and she kissed me gently. 'I admire tremendously your worldly knowledge and I think you are very astute. I also like the way you try to maintain good relations between me and your sons.'

She stopped and looked away. 'And . . . what else?' I said gently.

She kissed me again and continued. 'Sometimes, when Rory and Redmond were very rude to me I felt like packing my things and leaving.'

'Why didn't you?'

She smiled. 'Because I love you and want to be with you. Sometimes, though, I wonder if I should have left. I know I will be terribly frightened when we set sail. If I'd gone, my heart would be broken, but I would have got over that.'

'But you won't go now, will you?'

'I don't know, Gerald, I really don't. I like the way there is more friendship now between your sons and me and I like the way we are all working together in this adventure. That is nice.'

Gently I put my arms around her and she clutched me passionately.

'Please, let us never part,' she whispered. 'I never want to leave you.'

I hugged her tightly, reassuring her with kisses.

On the Sunday Jerry called with the good news that DAS had caught his potential kidnappers. I told him about the ceibo and asked if Plan, by any chance, had a chainsaw. 'We have two,' he said, 'but they are both broken and we are still waiting for new parts to come from Ecuador.' Hugo asked us to join him for drinks on the beach, although he was already well sozzled.

'What did you think of the people in the jungle?' Jerry asked me, when we were all a little tipsy.

'I liked them,' I said. 'A refreshing change from the town dwellers I have seen.'

'Like I told you, they are, in the main, nice, friendly people. Every race has its rogues – you know that. The negroes just need a chance to improve themselves in this world. They learn and adapt very quickly. And they have something most of us white people have lost: inherent, basic skills with their hands.'

'With that I agree,' I said. 'Those people in the jungle make a living where most city dwellers would give up and die. Another example of inherent basic skills is the Australian Aborigine. Put him in a desert and he'll survive by finding water, and roots to eat. He just knows where they are by instinct.'

We were discussing Man's present craving for city life and his sad neglect of all things rural when Hugo interrupted. 'You two are not drinking,' he accused us, sternly. 'No more serious talk, please. Let us drink.'

'We are drinking, Hugo,' I said. 'That's what's making me talk too much!'

Jerry laughed and toasted Hugo with his glass. 'Quite right, Hugo,' he said. 'We've been talking politics – and drink and politics don't mix.'

Turning to me, Jerry asked how we were managing for food.

'The last 6,000 you lent us has almost gone. Food's very dear here. But Alex has kindly offered to be our guarantor at one of the stores, so that's one thing I don't have to worry about.'

'If the store doesn't have anything you want,' said Jerry, 'I can arrange credit for you at the co-op. And, of course, you now have quite a nice house for free!' He sighed, ostentatiously. 'Sometimes I think I'm far too good to you people!'

'I think you are, too,' I said. 'I think I'll dedicate my book to you.'

'I don't want you to do that,' he said, seriously. 'Just write it and send me a free copy. I suggest you dedicate it to Yeannie and your two sons for going along with the ideas of a complete eccentric who has a very basic, black and white concept of this world and its problems.'

'Absolutely!' said Yeannie. 'Gerald is very juvenile, like a little boy at times, but very lovely.'

'We will drink to that,' slurred Hugo, though I'm sure he hadn't a clue what it was he was going to drink to.

On the Wednesday morning, Alex called us early to say he was going to the jungle, but we couldn't leave until nine because of the tide. By the time we reached Maximino's it had gone eleven. With the boys and me armed with an axe each – for Alex had also lent us one which was a bit ancient – we all set off for the ceibo in the sweltering heat, Maximino proudly pointing out the grave of the ekkiss.

On seeing the ceibo for the first time, Redmond exclaimed: 'Jesus Christ, Dad, we'll never fell that! It's fucking huge!'

'My son,' I said, like an Edwardian father, 'tell me news, not history. Of course it's fucking huge. And we are going to fell it.' I was about to add: 'Even if it kills me,' but thought better of it.

With a very pointed 'It's all yours' from Alex and a laugh from Maximino, the two of them left us to it. 'We'll bring you something to eat and drink in about two hours' time,' Alex shouted to us through the foliage.

After much walking around the trunk, assessing it, and cutting down a few smaller trees to let in more light, the boys and I selected a vane each. With the first cuts we all glanced apprehensively aloft to see if any flying snakes had decided to sod the sun with the vibrations and become airborne.

Within minutes our shirts and jeans were saturated with sweat. We took our shirts off, but had to put them back on almost immediately because the bites of the enormous mosquitoes – the biggest I'd ever seen – were more unbearable than the heat. Every now and then, we took photographs of the tree and ourselves with the camera Jerry had lent us, together with a roll of film.

I had gone to see him the day before to ask if he had a camera I could borrow. His attempt at sarcasm had been over-ridden by his humour. 'What sort of an author are you who doesn't have a camera? Now, are you sure you don't want me to take the photographs for you? And you're quite sure you know how to load the film?' I politely told him why I didn't have a camera. I had asked a professional cameraman in Quito to come to the Galapagos. 'When the Galapagos adventure proved a no-go, he left and I just never got round to buying one.'

Three vanes had been cut completely through when the handle of Alex's axe, which Rory was using, snapped in two. 'Never mind,' I said. 'One of us can always be resting while the other two chop.'

Two more vanes were almost severed when Alex and Maximino arrived with fish, rice, beans, bananas and three *pipas*. 'You're doing pretty good,' Alex encouraged us. He was unconcerned about the axe handle.

'What time is it?' I asked.

'Just two o'clock,' he said. 'You have four more hours. We will collect you at six. We want to be out of the jungle before dark.' Aside to me, he added: 'I have a big problem. I have to do more talking to the men in the village. The cheque for their work here from the shrimp company in Bogotá has not arrived, and the men are not very happy about it.'

When I mentioned this to the boys after Alex and Maximino had departed, Redmond commented: 'Tell them to join the club, Dad. We know what it's like, waiting for a cheque to arrive.'

'Are you sure we are going to do this today, Dad?' Rory asked, with some concern. 'I'm getting terrible blisters on both hands.' Redmond's hands were also blistered, and so were mine.

'Just keep going steadily,' I said. 'If we don't fell it today, we don't. It's as simple as that.'

120

An hour or so later, our blisters started to burst. We cut off the tails of our shirts and used them as bandages. We had left the sixth vane, which was on the side facing the cacaos and had cut the vee on the side where the bananas were. 'Do you think it will fall that way, Dad?' asked Redmond.

'I don't know which way the bloody thing will fall,' I said. 'The trunk is dead straight and doesn't lean in any direction. The branches, too, seem to be pretty evenly balanced. What we really need is a rope to pull it the way we want it to fall.'

We carried on, hacking out the trunk between the vanes. Rory, who had swung the axe with tremendous vigour during the first hours, was the first to tire. His face took on a pallor as his energy failed. Redmond, too, began constantly complaining of a pounding pain in his head. They took longer and longer rests. All our hands were bleeding. I carried on without resting.

'Dad, don't give yourself a heart attack,' said Rory. 'The bloody tree's not worth it.'

'I'm all right,' I said. 'Don't worry about me. I'll stop when I have to. Us old 'uns are always tougher than you young buggers.'

At six o'clock, when Alex and Maximino called for us, we were all absolutely knackered. I felt very disappointed and slightly angry that the tree wasn't on the ground. 'Another half an hour, that's all that's needed,' I told Alex. He picked up one of the axes and attacked the sixth vane. After several cuts, there came a tremendous 'crack' from the trunk. Alex dropped the axe and ran.

We all laughed. 'It will need a bit more chopping than that before it falls,' I said. 'Can you bring us back tomorrow?'

'Yes, I can tomorrow,' said Alex, 'but I don't think I'll be coming up again for a week or so after that. It depends if the cheque arrives. But Arthur has a canoe. I'm sure he would lend it to you.'

As we got into the dinghy I noticed that Rory's face was very peaky under his tan. 'Are you all right?' I asked.

'No, Dad,' he said. 'I feel ever so sick. I don't want anything to eat tonight. I just want to go to bed.'

The stars were shining when we emerged from Maximino's long, narrow creek into one of the main channels. The tide was running fairly high and against us, but the dinghy planed fast and smoothly. Rounding one of the islands we saw the searchlight's intermittent beam from the port captain's rock. Round another island and Tumaco's blaze of lights came into view and seemed welcoming and warm. Next to me, Rory was trying to doze. He didn't help us beach the dinghy but went straight to bed.

The next morning when I awoke the first thing I became conscious of was the pain in my fingers and palms. In the grey light filtering through the mosquito net, I studied my right hand. It had two large red-raw blisters, one on the palm next to the thumb, the other on the inside of the third joint of my third finger. Then I looked at the left. Five more blisters, all without skin and cracking through the hard scabs. To make matters worse, the backs of my hands were covered with itching mosquito bites.

As always, my movements woke Yeannie. She looked at my hands, and kissed them. The night before she had washed our shirt-tail bandages and put out the tube of Savlon that had accompanied us to the Galapagos. I got up and went to Redmond's bedroom which was the nearer. He instantly thrust his hands out from under the mosquito net for me to see. They were as bad as mine. 'How do you feel?' I asked him. 'Ready to knock that tree down?'

'Apart from a pain across my shoulders, excruciating agony in both hands, and the fact that I am dying, I feel perfectly well. Anyway, piss off – it's too early to get up.'

I went into Rory's bedroom. He was fast asleep. I gently shook him and he groaned. His hands, too, were very bad. 'I can't face the heat and the mosquitoes again today, Dad,' he said. 'I really can't. I just want to sleep and forget where we are and what we're doing.'

'All right,' I said. 'You sleep. Redmond and I can do it.'

122

Alex was waiting for us to help put the dinghy into the sea when Redmond and I went to the beach. 'Rory?' he asked. I told him that Rory was too sick. 'He always attacks any work too hard to start with,' I explained. 'Since he was a little boy I've always told him to take things easy, but he never listens. No one can work as fast as he did in this heat.'

When we reached Maximino's, Alex said he and Maximino were going off in the dinghy to another part of the jungle to talk to someone about timber for Maximino's new house. 'You'll be able to find the tree all right?' he asked.

'Yes,' I said. 'The trail's well marked.'

Redmond and I pussy-footed, with axes at the ready, through the clearing where the ekkiss lay, and without mishap, found our way to the ceibo. 'Bugger it,' said Redmond. 'It's still standing. I was hoping the wind might have blown it down in the night.'

The ceibo had moved slightly, though, and I could see that it had no intention of falling where Maximino wanted it to. Daubing Savlon on our palms and wrapping the bandages around, we set to with the axes. It was agony at first until the scabs on the blisters softened. Suddenly, the area darkened, the heavens opened and we were drenched and chilly in seconds. The cloud passed and the air was hotter than ever with the humidity, and the mosquitoes descended with whetted and wetted appetites. 'Do you think this fucking tree's worth it, Dad?' said Redmond, squashing a mosquito on his cheek.

'You want to go to England, don't you?'

'Yeah, but I keep having visions of sitting on a reclining seat and a beautiful air stewardess bringing me ice-cold rum and Coke. It's the only way to travel, Dad.'

'Just shut up and keep watching out. She'll go in a minute. You'd better come round this side with me. And don't forget what I've always told you. Don't run like Alex did. Keep close to the roots, so if the tree does swing at the last minute, you've got a shorter distance to dodge it.'

'You know that. I know that. But does the bloody tree know it?'

After what we estimated to be half an hour, the trunk gave an almighty crack, heralding its impending death. Then fibres began snapping like pistol shots. As the massive tree started to fall, with long, ear-splitting screeches of rending timber, it began twisting to the right. I grabbed Redmond's arm and pulled him to the left and back several feet now that I knew for sure which way the tree would go. Chunks of wood and large splinters flew into the air from the base as the tree accelerated in its descent. The noise it made was deafening. Then it hit the ground, sending a shock wave under our feet. The tremor was felt in the village, two kilometres away. Leaves and small pieces of debris floated and fell all around – then the jungle was deathly still once more.

Redmond hugged me with excitement. 'We've done it, Dad! We've done it! Cor, I wish Rory could have seen it. It was spectacular!' Then he laughed. 'But, of course, you got it wrong again, Dad. Look at all the cacao we've squashed!'

The trunk lay, like a giant, silvery-green pipeline, going off into the distance where it disappeared in a tangled mass of its own branches and those of mangled cacao trees. 'Poor old Maximino,' I said. 'I expect we'll have to give him some money for those.'

We climbed up on to the trunk and strode along its wide girth, pretending it was already our canoe. 'You stay one end, Dad, and I'll go to the other to get some perspective of what it will be like.' He stopped where the branches started, turned to me and waved. 'God! You're miles away, Dad,' he called. Then he assumed the air of a captain and walked to midships. 'Cast off, aft!' he commanded. 'Cast off, for'ard!'

'Come on,' I said, laughing, 'let's measure our new possession.'

Using a metal tape measure, we found that from the cut to the nearest branch was just over seventy-five feet! 'We'll have the longest canoe in the world, Dad,' he said.

'We won't,' I told him. 'Look at this split. It's about ten foot long, and there's another one at the other end. But forty foot is all we want, else we'll never be able to manoeuvre it.'

Next, we measured the circumference. At the thicker end it was 13 feet 7½ inches; at the point where the branches started, a little more than 12 feet. While I was assessing which side should be the keel, cutting away some of the clinging creepers, Redmond walked on along, through the branches to see what damage had been done to the cacaos. He soon came hurrying back, flailing his arms. 'Bees!' he shouted. 'Millions of 'em!'

'Well, don't come near me!' I shouted back. But only two or three had followed Redmond and these soon left him. They were the same shape as a bumble bee but smaller – and they were all black. I went along the trunk and peered through the branches. The air was black with them. 'We'd better keep down the other end,' I advised. 'They're not very happy about having their happy home smashed.'

We had stripped off quite a lot of creeper from the trunk and had marked a forty-foot section when Alex called for us to go back to Tumaco. On the journey, he seemed preoccupied and said very little except that he might not be going back to the jungle for about a week. It was March 29 – only thirty-nine days left in Colombia – so, that afternoon, I went to see Arthur. Yes, of course, we could borrow his canoe, but there was no engine. I asked Jerry if Plan had one to spare. 'We do have an old Yamaha 15 hp,' he said, 'but you'll have to wait a few days until my chief mechanic gets back because I don't know where it is or what state it's in.' I gave him a progress report about the ceibo.

Late next morning, Alex came round to see us. The cheque had arrived from Bogotá and he was going to the jungle after all. Would I like to go and talk business with Onofre?

I took Yeannie with me because she was better at speaking the language and could tell Onofre exactly what

I wanted. When the villagers first saw her, they asked if she was my daughter. When Yeannie told them we were married, there was much amusement and laughter and they called me a 'child bandit'!

Onofre went with us to look at the tree. Yeannie couldn't believe its size, and that we had felled it in such a short time with only axes. She told Onofre that I didn't want it flat-bottomed, like all the other canoes, but with a keel. He said he would like to carve the bow; it was his speciality and it would cut the water like a knife. Yeannie asked how many days would his work take. 'Seven,' he replied, 'if you cut the trunk to size and take out the middle ready for me to scoop it out smooth.'

'How will we get the canoe to the water when it is finished?' Yeannie asked, killing a large mosquito on her bare arm.

Onofre scratched his head. 'A lot of weight,' he said, eventually. 'I think it will need twenty-five men to pull it. But we have that many in the village. You must bring a very long, strong rope.'

On the walk back to the village, I asked Yeannie what she thought of the tree. 'It's beautiful,' she said, 'and I think it will make a beautiful boat. But how can you work in this heat and with all the mosquitoes? Look! My arms are covered with bites! And the thought of all those snakes! Ugh! I don't think I care very much for the jungle.'

I then asked her what she thought of the villagers. 'They appear friendly,' she said, 'but I think they could easily kill someone. Their eyes are very cold and I can understand why there are so many murders. I feel frightened of them.'

We suddenly reached a three-strand, barbed-wire fence where the jungle abruptly gave way to an expanse of thick, ankle-deep grass. Across the clearing, we could see the wooden huts of the village clustered round a creek black with mud now that the tide was out. Lofty, umbrella-like heads of coconut palms drooped in the stillness, affording some shade to the parched, grass-thatched roofs. Here and there, variegated cattle grazed or lay, drowsily chewing the cud, in the verdant, sun-sparkling lushness. Onofre pressed down the middle strand of the fence with his machete and raised the top one with his hand for Yeannie and me to duck through. We did the same for him.

'I would never like to live here,' Yeannie continued. 'It is too hot with the humidity and there are too many mosquitoes and poisonous snakes. I shall be very happy to leave Tumaco and Colombia. I would like very much for us one day to go back to Quito and visit Lucho and Ana. They are lovely people and Quito is a beautiful city.'

It was ten long, wasted and frustrating days before the boys and I could get back to the jungle. Jerry had told us that according to his mechanic, the Yamaha 15 hp was in bits and there were several parts missing. Alex spent most days with his cockerels and seemed to have lost interest in the jungle project. When he wasn't attending to the cockerels, he concerned himself with a new house that was being built for him and Sonia in Tumaco proper.

One evening he invited Rory to go to the cockfight with him. Next morning, at breakfast – because he didn't get back until the early hours – he told us about it.

First came the parade of fighting cocks round an open-air arena which had about fifty ringside seats, absolutely jammed solid with two or even three people in each seat. The betting started immediately after the cocks had been paired according to weight and age. An owner could value his bird for as much as 80,000 pesos and when that ante had been reached the fight became a fixture. If insufficient money was betted the owner withdrew his cockerel. The judge held all the money. All the cockerels had nude legs. Feathers were plucked to keep them cooler. Sharp-pointed talons of tortoise-shell were then strapped to the cockerels' legs, and they fought with those and their beaks. Each talon was examined by the judge and his aides before the fight, stuck into an orange and wiped clean to ensure the owner wasn't using poison.

Maximum time for each fight was half an hour, but many times the fight ended before that when one opponent fell dead or exhausted, or the owner took it out because

127

it was getting the worst of it. Whenever an artificial talon became jammed inside the flesh of a bird, the judge stopped the fight, counted to five and the fight continued.

'It doesn't sound much like my idea of sport,' I commented. 'Did you enjoy it?'

'Not much,' he said, 'but I had a helluva lot to drink! Alex won a fair bit of money and he was almost legless. I drove the motorcycle back.'

'I bet Rory really enjoyed it, Dad,' said Redmond. 'Remember when you took us to the bullfight in Ronda in Spain? Mum, Roddick and me felt sick and closed our eyes every time the matador killed the bull.'

'Rory didn't?' queried Yeannie.

'No,' I said. 'The blood-thirsty little sod enjoyed every minute of it.'

Just when we were becoming very despondent about everything – there was no news of my money, either – Alex cheered us up by saying he was going to fetch Maximino very early the next morning to help with Alex's new house. We would be able to have a full day on the tree. Our hands were healed and by the nightfall we had cut off both ends. To our joy, Alex went to Maximino's again on the following day. Onofre came over to see us as we were stripping off more of the creeper. He went back to the village and returned with two other men to help roll the giant trunk so that the part we wanted as the top was uppermost. They also cut down and cleared a wide area on each side of the trunk. Alex and Maximino appeared on the scene late in the afternoon, and the latter wasn't at all concerned about his cacao. In fact, he took one of the axes and helped to strip off the heavy, thick bark.

Maximino also told us that Alex was coming up again on the 13th – three days' time – and again on the 15th. If we stayed at his house for the two nights we would have three days' uninterrupted work on the trunk. I thanked him very much and he asked us to bring blankets and some food because he wasn't very rich.

'I couldn't face two nights sleeping up there,' said Yeannie when I told her about Maximino's offer. 'But,' she wailed, 'it will be the first time we haven't slept together!'

'Well you can't stay in this house alone for two nights,' I said. So Yeannie went to see Mercedes and she immediately agreed that Yeannie should sleep there.

'I don't know what food to take,' I told Yeannie the night before we were to leave.

'Rice and beans mix with anything,' she said. 'And coffee and sugar are quite dear, so take those as well. It will be a nice gesture. Also, a couple of tins of tinned meat and a tin of powdered milk.'

'It's a good job we have accounts at the store and co-op,' I said.

Obviously, Maximino and his wife were very pleased with the goodies, for they decided to give us a treat, too, for our first evening meal. We were invited up to the second floor where I had eaten previously. The table had been nicely laid, and there were glasses and a big jug of fruit juice. The rice had been cooked with onions and the beans had been made into a rich sauce.

Maximino poured us each a glass of juice and told us to help ourselves to the rice and sauce. His wife put a bowl of boiled bananas on the table, and we thought that was it. But no.

Beaming with absolute pride and pleasure, in which Maximino joined, too, the woman placed a large black roasting tray on the table. On it were four large roasted rats, flat like kippers. Their long, pointed mouths were open, showing the rows of needle-sharp teeth. The heat had caused their long tails to coil round and round like Catherine wheels.

I decided not to look at Rory and Redmond.

We sat in silence as the woman, with her hands, tore off a back leg and placed it on my plate. She did the same for the boys and Maximino. Following his example, I picked the leg up with my fingers. I gave it a brief sniff. It smelled like rabbit. I took a small nibble. It *was* like rabbit, but with a strong, pungent after-taste. With many spoonfuls of rice, beans and banana in between, I managed

129

to eat it all. I saw that Redmond was also eating his. But Rory carefully left his on the plate.

'You don't like it?' asked Maximino. 'I eat it for you.' And he did.

That night as we slept, rolled in our blankets on the kitchen floor, rats skipped and played merrily around us. The family slept together in one big room downstairs.

'Now I've got rat outside me as well as inside me,' groaned Redmond. Rory had told me quietly after dinner that if he had taken one mouthful, he would have spewed instantly. 'How could you and Redmond eat it?' And he had shuddered.

As I lay, trying to sleep on the hard, dirty floor, I kept telling myself that I had eaten rabbit not rat and there was no necessity to be sick!

Thankfully, on the following night we had crab, and for lunch there was always fish. The first thing Rory told Yeannie on our return was that Redmond and I had eaten rat. 'Ugh!' she exclaimed. 'You scrub your teeth three times before you kiss me!'

'But that was two days ago,' I objected.

'I don't care,' she said. 'Clean your teeth. The thought of eating rat is disgusting!'

Three days later, Alex took materials for Maximino's house. I went with him to talk to Onofre and see when he could start on the trunk. The boys and I had stripped off most of the bark and had taken a lot out of the centre. Onofre went with me to the trunk and he nodded his head with satisfaction at our work. 'I will start in two days' time,' he said. 'First I will do the bow and keel.'

'There's one thing I don't like about this trunk,' I told him. 'Look. It has a soft centre.'

'No problem,' he assured me. 'It will be necessary for you to seal it with tar. Come. We will go to my father's house to wait for Alex.'

The house was a fair distance from the village and, like the village houses, was next to a wide sea channel. We crossed a stream by means of a fallen tree and walked through a long meadow by the side of the water and through a large herd of Brahmin cattle. 'These are my father's,' he said, proudly.

'It's a beautiful spot here,' I congratulated him, and I really meant it. The first thing I noticed about the house was the absence of rubbish around it; and the inside was very clean. Onofre's sister had the running of the household. She was as tall as her brother, full-breasted and quite beautiful. Her hair was nicely done and her blue floral dress had the appearance of being ironed.

The kitchen, what I could see of it, was neat and tidy, with folded clean linen on the table. Saucepans were hung along one wall, their bottoms and sides shining like new. Showing a lovely set of white teeth in a smile of welcome, Onofre's sister asked me if I would like something to eat. 'Yes,' I said. 'Thank you.'

She obviously had a meal ready, for she quickly produced a plate of rice with a nice piece of chicken on top. After I'd eaten it, I thanked her again, adding that the chicken was delicious. She looked at her brother and they both laughed.

'That wasn't chicken,' she said. 'That was an animal of the jungle.'

'Not snake?' I exclaimed.

'No,' she replied, still laughing. 'It was tortoise.'

Never in my wildest dreams would I ever have thought tortoise would taste as good as that. No wonder the pirates and other sailors took on board the giant tortoises of Galapagos, almost to extinction, to keep themselves supplied with 'excellent' meat on their voyages.

I told Onofre and his sister about the Galapagos tortoise. 'When they stand up straight, they are as high as a person's waist,' I said. 'And when they stretch up their long necks they could take a leaf off your shoulder.'

'Didn't you kill any and eat them?' asked Onofre.

'No,' I said. 'They are protected now by law, and there weren't any where we were. The ones I saw were kept on a big farm where they can breed without the rats eating their eggs. The rats, of course, were taken to the islands

131

by the ships. When the young tortoises are big enough to defend themselves against the rats, they are put into their natural habitats – the large, muddy pools on top of the extinct volcanoes.'

I was telling them about the pink flamingoes on the islands when Onofre's father arrived, carrying a bottle of Aguardiente. He was shorter than his children and wiry. His hair was turning grey and his beard stubble was almost all white. He told me he had once been a merchant seaman and had seen several countries. 'Now, I am happy to be a farmer,' he added, mixing the Aguardiente with the juice of a *pipa* his daughter had brought in. She didn't join us but took a big bundle of clothes to the nearby fresh-water hole where she was joined by two more women from a lone neighbouring house. And there they sat, laughing and talking, sometimes sharing a cigarette as they washed their clothes. Alex and two young villagers arrived, each carrying a bottle of Aguardiente. It looked like being another session!

Everyone wanted to know how the boat was coming along and when it would be ready to be pulled to the water. I asked how much they thought I should pay the men for doing the pulling. 'A crate of Aguardiente,' said Onofre's father, refilling my glass. 'You say it will take twenty men besides yourselves. There are twelve bottles in a crate – more than half a bottle each – and we can all have a big celebration afterwards!'

We all drank to that. 'Where is your lovely young wife today?' asked Onofre's father. 'I would like to see her. I think you must have a very big prick for her to marry a man twice her age. But all you gringos have big pricks.'

'Is that true?' the two younger men asked.

'Oh, yes,' said Onofre's father. 'When I was in the navy I saw many gringos' pricks.' He measured about nine inches to a foot between his hands. 'This big! Oh, yes,' nodding his head, solemnly, 'all gringos have big pricks. Everyone knows that. Much bigger than a black man's. Isn't that so, gringo?'

I decided to be enigmatic and simply smiled. What a

turn-up for the books, I thought. Many white men believed the myth that black men were the better endowed despite medical evidence to the contrary, and here was the same myth, only in reverse. Onofre's father was still going on about the different sizes he had seen on white men – all quite huge – when his neighbour arrived. He was about the same age as Onofre's father and he confirmed everything that was being said.

Everyone regarded me with great respect and, with the alcohol inside me, I assumed a superior air! The conversation became quite obscene before it was exhausted.

Onofre's father was very interested in the boat project and he wanted to know my proposed route to England.

'I will follow the Colombian coast right up to Panama,' I said. 'From there to the Grand Cayman, which is British, on to Miami, then up the coast to New York and on to Newfoundland, the route that the old sailing ships always took. Then, of course, there's the 3,000 miles of Atlantic to cross – but I'm not too worried about that. It's already been done by two men in a rowing boat.'

The old boy thought the route a good and sensible one. 'You will have to watch for cyclones in the Caribbean and you'll need a guide to get out of Tumaco. Whew! the waves are colossal! And don't hug the Colombian coast too much. Shallows cause giant waves nearly all the way to Panama.'

Two days later, when I knew that Onofre was going to start work and there was still no news of my money, I told Jerry I was getting very worried. He handed me the phone, saying: 'Be my guest. Phone your bank.' I did so after Arthur had taken me on his motorcycle to get my address book. Remembering previous difficulties and delays when phoning from abroad, I was pleasantly astonished when the bank in Bromyard answered almost immediately. The manager was away, but the assistant manager assured me that the cheque for £1,000 payable to a Jerry Vink had been cleared more than a week ago.

'I know what has probably happened,' said Jerry, after

133

I had told him. 'My bank is in Canada and all my money comes from there to this bank. I bet these people here sent your cheque to Canada to be posted on to England and it's gone back to Canada first before being sent on here. But still, you know that the cheque has been received and paid by your bank. I reckon it should be here any day now. Also, I have some more good news for you: my chief mechanic has located another old Yamaha 15 hp you can borrow. He's working on it now. You should be able to collect it in a couple of days.'

The boys and Yeannie were overjoyed when I told them the two good pieces of news. 'Things might start happening now, then, Dad,' said Redmond. They certainly did – the very next day, but not what we were expecting.

At mid-day, Alex said he was taking more material up to Maximino's, would I like to go with him for company and see if Onofre had started on the trunk. Yeannie and the boys had already planned an afternoon lazing on the beach with Mercedes and Sonia. Hugo had gone off to a government conference in Bogotá for five days.

It was quite dark when Alex and I got back. Everyone came hurrying down the beach, babbling about a fire. 'Can you smell the burning?' Yeannie asked, in great distress. 'I have been very afraid. I thought the house was going to be burned to the ground.' I could see she was very upset.

'What on earth has happened?' I asked. Alex had asked the same sort of question for his mother was talking rapidly to him in near-hysteria.

'That poxy negro neighbour set fire to the grass,' said Rory, 'and, of course, the wind's in this direction. We've had quite an exciting time.'

'Is the house damaged?'

'No,' said Redmond. 'But now he can see our house and we can see his. Yeannie, the little fart, nearly shit herself. She was in the house alone – we were out on the raft.'

'I don't think there was any danger, Dad,' said Rory, phlegmatically.

134

'What do you mean, no danger?' Yeannie said, angrily. 'The flames were higher than the house. Your sons are stupid!'

'Now, come on,' I said, 'calm down. What did you do?'

'Rory and Redmond threw buckets of water over the verandah and side of the house,' she said. 'But not until I had screamed at them to do so.'

'And what did you do?' sneered Redmond. 'Stayed, cowering on the beach.'

'I did not,' she declared, defiantly. 'I was the one who threw water on to the grass.'

'Oh, shut up, the lot of you,' I said. 'Bicker, bicker, bicker, that's all you do. Anyway, why didn't someone call the fire brigade?'

'Because there's no fucking telephone,' said Rory.

'I thought the Benitezes had one.'

'No,' said Yeannie, 'the nearest one is at Plan.'

Alex had gone into his house and he came back onto the verandah with his pistol. He fired it twice over our roof at the negro's house. Seconds later there came two red flashes and answering reports. Alex fired twice more, and again the negro returned fire.

'They're bloody silly kids,' I snorted. 'What the hell do they think they can do at that range?'

As though to signal an end to the minor barrage, all the lights went out with the usual electricity cut.

'Ah, well,' I said, as we walked up the beach, 'I just hope the water's still on – I feel grubby.'

My body was covered with soap when the water went off. Yeannie threw two buckets of water over me from the outside wash tubs. Over a candle-lit dinner I told them that Onofre was working very hard on the trunk. That night in bed I related the conversation with Onofre's father and his belief about gringos.

'I would say that Onofre's father knows what he is talking about,' she said, giggling.

Next morning I got up and looked through the bedroom window. 'It certainly looks different,' I commented. 'It's like the Russian scorched earth policy.'

135

'What is that?' she asked. So I explained.

The negro's house was clearly visible across the acre or so of black ground. Wisps of smoke were rising from clumps and odd pieces of wood. As is usual with grass fires, the trees were scorched and black round their trunks but in no way dead. The house – or rather bungalow – was similar to ours and looked quite clean and tidy. As I watched through the window, a young man and woman came out, looking very smartly dressed. They got on to an almost new motorcycle and rode off. The negro, also very well dressed and accompanied by two dogs, appeared and waved to them. He glanced once in our direction and went back inside. He didn't at all represent the picture the Benitezes had given of a crazy, mad, bad man; and I couldn't help wondering what the true situation was. Judging by the two cars standing outside, the motorcycle and overall appearance, the negro looked to me like a man of wealth.

12

Arthur's canoe was like the walls of Maximino's shack: aged and full of holes. But it floated and – it was transport! The Yamaha 15 was also the worse for wear. Plan's chief mechanic, a young black man, was trying to start it outside the wharf workshop when all four of us arrived to collect our new possession.

There isn't much I don't know about two-stroke engines, especially outboards, and there are few things so cantankerous as an old and worn one. My policy with the Torres Strait islanders' engines, when they brought them to me for repair, was always to strip them down completely; for if I just repaired or rectified, say, the ignition system, ten-to-one the petrol system or gears would go up the creek in a day or so, and back the engine would come with a dissatisfied customer.

I instantly saw that the Yamaha's plugs were rusty and dirty, and I suggested to the mechanic that he put in new ones. He replied that there weren't any. The parts order hadn't arrived from Ecuador.

The choke mechanism was also faulty and the connecting rod to the knob on the lid was missing, which meant that the lid had to be removed to apply the choke. It needed two people to start the engine because the throttle linkage was badly worn and wouldn't stay in the correct position when the starter cord was pulled. I held the throttle lever while the mechanic pulled the cord, and the engine started. After the cloud of blue smoke had dissipated, the engine ticked over quite nicely, provided I kept my hand on the throttle.

The mechanic got out of the canoe. Yeannie and the boys got in and sat on the rim so that there were two of us on one side and two on the other for balance.

'Hurry up, Dad,' urged Rory. 'The heat is terrific. Let's get some breeze.'

The mechanic untied the anchor rope, I put the engine into gear and opened the throttle slowly as I had no wish to strain or break anything. We were a fair old weight for a 15 horsepower engine until momentum assisted it. Off we went to the petrol station with a credit chit signed by Jerry. Gradually, I opened the throttle to 'Full', the engine responding well, and the bow sending the spray high on both sides. The canoe was about twenty feet long and less than two feet wide, causing it to roll, especially at low speed. But we'd had practice before with a canoe's roll.

A little way up the main road from our house lived a young, one-legged negro who had a wife and family. His only livelihood was fishing. So, in an act of philanthropy the Benitezes had bought a small canoe for him. It was only about twelve feet long and just wide enough for buttocks to fit between the sides. Paddle was the only power, as was the case with all the poor negroes' canoes. The Benitezes allowed him to anchor it on their beach. It had looked so simple to us as we'd watched the one-legged man hop down the beach with his crutch, sit himself in the canoe and paddle away. We had become friendly with him, and always one of us would push his canoe down to the water at low tide. In return, he said we could use the canoe for fishing.

I got into it first, settled myself and the boys pushed me out. Immediately, the damn thing overturned! Yeannie and the boys all had goes – and all went overboard. 'How come the dug-out you built on Cocos wasn't like this?' asked Redmond, getting up out of the water.

'Probably because it was heavier wood and was vee-bottomed instead of flat, causing it to sit lower in the water,' I said.

We persevered and after a week were able to balance and go across to the uninhabited island to fish, usually with Rory and Redmond in the canoe, towing Yeannie and me on the bamboo raft. One day Rory and I decided to venture the two kilometres to the store by canoe so that we didn't have to cross the bridge which was always crowded with men out of work and suffer the stares of them and all the others along the street.

Because the bridge was so narrow, the current was quite strong each time the lagoon emptied and filled with the tides. Forgetting about that, Rory and I paddled gracefully and slowly up to the bridge. The current was against us and, with the idlers looking on and laughing, it stopped us, swung us round and sent us back the way we had come.

'Bastard!' I exclaimed. 'Right, Rory. Let's get up some speed to beat the current.' We did so, and hit the current head-on. Gradually we slowed, then we were able to get our hands on the pillars to pull us through. Two laughing children jumped in and pushed us – and we were out on the other side to the accompaniment of laughter and hoorays!

'Whichever way we go, we get stared at,' grumbled Rory.

But now we had a decent canoe and wouldn't have to worry which way the current was going. Being me, I forgot about something else as I sped the canoe up to the wharf of the petrol station. I had been used to planing craft which, whenever the throttle is closed, stopped almost dead, the water acting as a brake as the craft sinks into it. Not so a canoe. It keeps on going! We were going at quite a lick, too, when I closed the Yamaha's throttle. Everyone shouted as we came speeding in. I steered the canoe so that the side of the bow would hit the nearest pillar and we'd slide along all of them to brake us. The boys also tried grabbing the pillars. But the weight of momentum was too much for them and we bounced off and went sailing on past.

Rather shame-faced, I turned the canoe around and went back in, very slowly, without mishap. 'Good,' said the attendant. 'I'm pleased you made it the second time.'

'Christ!' growled Rory. 'When are you ever going to get things right, Dad?'

'It was pretty good, I think,' I said, casually. 'Think what I'll be able to do with our 40-footer!'

139

'Yeah,' said Redmond. 'Take the wharf away!'

With five gallons of mix in the tank we went on down to the store and parked expertly in a small gap between other canoes. I was able to use the engine in reverse so that the bow lightly touched the shore – something I hadn't dared do at the filling station in case the back of the old canoe was torn away. I'd really got the feel of it when we reached the bridge on the way back. I'd had to make many twists and turns to avoid other craft and pieces of wood and other debris.

To the accompaniment of a short little scream from Yeannie, I went under the bridge at full throttle, heeled the canoe over to port at a crazy angle to avoid the big sandbank and sped on to our house. Rory and Redmond gave me the thumbs up sign of great approval.

It felt really good to be back on a boat again in control of the engine. Like a little boy, I wished I had the aluminium dinghy with the 40 hp Mariner on the back that I'd had in the Torres Strait. Then I'd show these people what speed was really like.

Naturally, Rory and Redmond wanted to try their hands at steering and quickly found it wasn't as easy as it looked. When the wheel of a road vehicle is turned, it is the front that moves round; but with a boat the front end wants to stay on a straight course, and it is the rear end that moves round – quite confusing to anyone who is used only to a car or motorcycle as the boys were. Several times, I saw Redmond lean his body over as he did on his motorcycle to turn the canoe, but of course to no avail and he hit the beach, or one of the piles left from an old wharf. Also I had to shout at them several times not to open the throttle on a sharp turn or the engine would roll the canoe clean over.

It was Rory's first attempt that caused the most laughter and amusement. The throttle was very tricky and he opened it too much to start off. He just managed to save himself from being jerked backwards into the water. Then, in a state of flummox but with the presence of mind to close the throttle – but to such an extent that the engine cut

140

dead – he was heading for the spot where some of the old wharf's piles were submerged. The bottom of the canoe struck one, slid along it to the centre of the canoe, and there the canoe hung, turning slowly with the current like a Spinning Jenny.

'Help me, Dad!' he cried.

'No! Bugger you!' I shouted back. 'You got into the situation – you get yourself out. It's good practice for you.'

A look of determination came over his face. He took off the lid and applied the choke. 'Put it out of gear first, Rory!' I called to him sharply. He did so, pulled the cord and the engine started first go. But the Yamaha hadn't the power to move the canoe forwards or backwards, though it did spin him round a bit faster on the pivot! He stopped the engine and scratched his head as we all sat ourselves on the beach to watch.

Using the oar – which was standard equipment in all canoes – he levered the canoe off sideways. We all gave him a cheer. He re-started the engine, put it into gear and went slowly out across the lagoon. Then he turned and came speeding back to the beach, opening the throttle all the time. When he was still a way out, he cut the engine and put it out of gear. Even so, the front half of the canoe came out of the water on to the beach close to where we were sitting.

'Pretty good, I think,' he said, happily. 'But I see what you mean, Dad; you need a helluva long distance to stop!'

'I think you really can handle a boat, Dad,' said Redmond, after his first attempt. 'Alex never goes under the bridge as fast as you did.'

'Naturally,' I said, blowing on my finger-nails in an act of complete and utter modesty.

'Oh,' said Yeannie, 'it's really nice having our own boat. No more having to walk all that way to Plan or the store – and no more waiting for Alex to go to the jungle.'

The outboard and petrol were taken into the house so that they wouldn't be stolen overnight. Next morning, while Yeannie and I poured boiled water into bottles to take with us, Rory and Redmond put the outboard back on the canoe and connected the petrol hose. Then we locked the doors and set off for the jungle. After we had passed the muck and wood floating off Tumaco's shoreline, the sea was clean and sparkling; but it was never clear because of the continuous disturbance by the tides of the silt and mud.

Opposite the lighthouse we turned right between two large, mangrove-covered islands. Some half an hour later we entered a narrower channel which resembled a muddy river in the Congo with its thick walls of mangroves on either side. Adding to that picture were the half-clad negroes that we encountered in their small, unpainted and paddle-driven canoes. Always, as courtesy, a motorised canoe was throttled back on passing so that the wake didn't buck the small canoes too much. And always, the four gringos in the motorised canoe received stares of surprise and curiosity!

'Look! Yeannie,' I said, pointing. 'A cockatoo.'

She smiled and nodded. 'It is really beautiful and peaceful here,' she said.

As I suddenly swung the canoe to the right to enter a narrow creek, she instantly enquired: 'Where are we going?'

'To Maximino's,' I told her. 'Oh, of course, we didn't go this way the last time you were with me.'

'It's very narrow and winding,' she said. I eased back the throttle. Several times the boys had to push us away from the crab-crawling muddy banks on the sharper bends. 'Are you going to bring our boat this way?' she asked, with some obvious doubt.

I nodded. 'Maximino is confident that it will be no trouble at high tide. The banks are wider at the top, so the bends won't be so sharp. At the moment, it's almost low tide.' To prove my last statement, I had to lift up the engine and punt the canoe the last fifty metres. Then we had the ordeal of wading through ankle-deep, black mud.

Maximino was away in the jungle, seeing to his rat traps; so, after a brief conversation with his wife, we collected the axes and set off for the ceibo.

142

With his usual teasing, Redmond pushed Yeannie ahead of us as we approached the grave of the ekkiss. 'This is where Maximino killed the Kiss of Death,' Redmond told her. 'And we've nominated you to see if its mate is there!' She gave a little squeak, ducked under his hand and ran back to me. 'He's only joking,' I said. 'The boys will go ahead.'

Onofre wasn't at the tree but a lot more wood had been taken out of the centre and the bow was taking shape. He'd obviously been there that morning because two small fires were still giving off smoke to ward off the mosquitoes. We worked for several hours and then decided we were starving.

'Let's go to Onofre's father's house to see if we can get something to eat,' I suggested. 'I know the trail and we can also find out what's happened to Onofre.'

When we reached the big meadow where the Brahmins were, we saw Onofre hurrying to the house. We shouted but he didn't hear. As we neared the house, dogs began barking excitedly. Then, looking like the Wild Man of Borneo, Onofre's father ran, shrieking, from the front door, brandishing a shotgun. Behind him ran Onofre and two other villagers, all waving machetes and yelling. They charged right past us as though we weren't there, the two dogs yapping at their heels. They were still running and shouting when they disappeared into the jungle at the far side of the meadow.

'What the hell was that all about?' asked Rory, letting the breath go from his body. We had all been a bit shaken.

'I don't know,' I said. 'It was as though they had worked themselves up to a fighting pitch like soldiers do when they fix bayonets and charge. One thing's for sure, I wouldn't like to be the poor buggers on the receiving end!'

'I told you that I thought these people were wild and could easily kill,' said Yeannie.

'And I think you're right,' I told her.

'Dad, the sooner we get that trunk finished and get back to our beach, the better,' said Redmond. 'These people are bloody maniacs. Did you see the look in their eyes? The old man's eyeballs looked red to me.'

Onofre's sister explained to us what it was all about. Someone, probably from another village, had not only stolen fish from their nets but had added insult to injury by taking the nets as well.

'What will your father and brother do if they catch him?' asked Yeannie.

'Kill him, of course,' she replied, quite matter-of-factly, as though it were the most natural thing in the world. 'I will get you something to eat – you must be very hungry for it is nearly three o'clock.' She hesitated. 'I would appreciate it, though, if you could give me 200 pesos for the rice, because we have to buy that.'

I looked at Redmond and he dug his hand into his jeans pocket. There were only 250 pesos – all the money we had left – and he gave her all of it.

'Are we having more animal of the jungle?' I asked her.

'No,' she said, laughing. 'We still have some fish left.'

With our bellies full of rice, fish and fruit juice, we took our leave. Thanking her very much I asked her to please tell her brother to continue working on the canoe as soon as possible because we had little time left in Colombia. She nodded. 'He works very hard,' she said. 'It is only because of this upset he is not working.'

We cut a lot more wood out of the centre and left the jungle when the sun started to dip below the tops of the trees. Arthur's canoe was floating and had about three inches of water in the bottom of it. The boys baled it out with two halves of coconut shell as we went along.

Jerry had just arrived as we got to the house. 'I thought I'd call by with the good news,' he said. 'Your money has arrived.'

'Yippee!' chorused Yeannie, Rory and Redmond.

'I think that calls for a glass or two of rum,' I said. 'Come on into the house.'

'I think I might be forced into doing just that.'

With the knowledge that we had money at last, the happiness was infectious. The rum also helped. We were, as Jerry said, quite rich. The exchange rate was 155 pesos to the pound, so, less a small bank commission, we had 153,766 pesos. Jerry thought it would be safer if he kept the money in his bank and drew it out as we wanted it. We agreed with that.

'Come to the office tomorrow morning at ten, and we'll sort it out,' he said. 'By the way, I've been thinking, you people should have a shotgun. The sea isn't the only thing that is dangerous between here and Buenaventura. Lots of pirates operate in those waters. Also, when your boat is nearly ready, two of you should sleep on board with the shotgun or you may lose everything. When you get your shotgun, have it with you on the beach in daytime so that people can see it and pass the message around that the gringos are armed.'

We sat talking and drinking for more than an hour. Then the lights went out. 'I think that's my cue to leave,' said Jerry. 'See you tomorrow.'

The next day we paid off all our debts, and I got my typewriter back from a very pleased Señora de Lopez. 'I wish you all the luck in the world and a very safe voyage,' she said.

As soon as I saw Alex, I asked him about the old Johnson 33 hp he said he would let us have. It was in a local shop for repair and I had agreed to pay the repair bill for it.

'I will go and see about it this evening,' he promised.

For three consecutive days, the boys and I went to the jungle in Arthur's canoe. On the first day, we learned from Onofre that the fish robber hadn't been caught. On the third day, the canoe was ready. As Redmond said: 'Gosh! It's really beautiful. And it's ours! Do you think they'll believe us in the Hop Pole when we tell them about this, Dad? How we cut the tree down with axes, with poisonous snakes and mosquitoes all around us?'

'We have photographs to prove it,' I told him. 'And photographs don't lie.'

I asked Onofre when the men would be ready to drag it to the river. 'The day after tomorrow,' he said.

145

'Tomorrow I will cut the path. You bring my money and the Aguardiente? And please don't forget the rope.'

'Of course,' I said. 'I'll buy the liquor and rope tomorrow.' We shook hands with him and left, agreeing that we would meet at the tree at ten o'clock on Sunday. It would then be April 28.

'Do you realise, Dad,' said Rory, 'that we'll only have eleven days to build the sides, put on a mast and paint all of it? – and we don't have an engine or a sail.'

'I know,' I said, grimly. 'We've really got our work cut out. But there are four of us – Yeannie says she wants to do the painting. And she's going to sew a sail out of flour sacks. We'll spend all day tomorrow buying everything we need. We'll make the list tonight.'

'And don't forget,' Redmond reminded me, 'we have to register the boat and get our permission to leave.'

13

No one left a canoe or boat unattended in Tumaco when
the engine and petrol were on board or, as quick as a flash,
they would be stolen. On the first trip in to buy things in
the morning, Yeannie stayed in the canoe. On the second
trip in the afternoon, Redmond said he would sit in the
canoe because he wanted to finish one of the paperbacks
Jerry had lent us. What with one thing and another, and
going to different shops to compare prices, we were away
quite a long time. When we returned to the canoe,
Redmond was more than relieved to see us. 'I've got a
terrible headache and I feel sick,' he said. 'It's very hot,
sitting in this sun.'

He didn't help to unload any of the things but went
straight to bed. Yeannie took him a cup of coffee when
everything was safely in the house, but he was asleep. I
awoke him for dinner, but he said he just wanted to sleep.
He did get up, though – to be sick.

As I had rightly guessed, he was in no fit state to go
with us to the jungle in the morning. So just Rory and I
went. It was ten thirty when we got to the ceibo. There
was no sign of anybody, but a wide trail had been cut,
heading straight for where we knew there was a grove of
coconuts. We had only the rope – thirty metres of it – for
Maximino had advised us to leave the crate of Aguardiente
at his place, or the men might drink it first and be incapable
of pulling anything!

'Just for curiosity's sake, while we're waiting,' I said, 'I
want to measure how far it is to the creek. Better hide the
rope under a bush.'

After Rory had done so, I told him I would stride it,
counting up to a hundred and he would keep a record of
the hundreds.

At the 150 mark, the trail entered the coconut grove where the undergrowth was sparse and had needed very little cutting. But the next 100 paces after the trail left the grove certainly made up for it. It was dense bush, similar to privet and very hard wood. 'Onofre has certainly earned 1,000 pesos if he cut this trail in a day,' said Rory.

Just after the 300 mark, the bush gave way to shoulder-high grass which continued for another seventy-five paces before turning into marshland. The land rose gradually and once more was bush-covered and dotted with large trees. At the top of the rise we could see the creek, and Maximino's shack about 150 metres further on from that.

'I make it 550 long paces,' I said. 'That's more than half a kilometre. Quite a way to lug one and a half tons.'

Taking our bearings, we could see that our normal trail to the ceibo from Maximino's and the trail for the boat formed almost an equilateral triangle. 'That's about right, Dad,' said Rory. 'I always reckoned it was a good kilo-metre to the tree. Let's get back – they should be there now.'

But they weren't. 'Where the devil are they?' I said, in exasperation. 'Onofre estimated it would take three hours to get to the creek. What's the time now? Quarter past eleven? We're going to miss that two o'clock tide. Bastard people! Why can't they do as they say they're going to do?'

'Well, *we* were half an hour late, Dad,' Rory pointed out, 'and Onofre's bound to show up – if only for his money!' He handed me a cigarette and we lit up. 'I think we've got a lovely boat, Dad. That bow is beautiful.'

I had to agree with him, despite my impatience.

'Yes, but it's not much good to us, sitting in the middle of the jungle. Do you realise that if Onofre can't get the men to help, we're absolutely buggered. And I bet he asks for more money, because he knows he's got us over a barrel.'

'Have you decided yet what name you're going to regis-ter it under?' he asked, running his hand along the smooth rim.

148

'Like I said originally – *The Islander*, after my book. Is that a small crack there?'

He looked where I was pointing. 'No. It's the grain. I still think the *Long John Thomas* would be a far better name, and these buggers here wouldn't know what it meant.'

'But people in England will – and if we do get there I can just imagine what the newspapers would say.'

'I think everybody would appreciate it,' he insisted. 'And it looks more like a long John Thomas than an islander.'

It did, too. It was 40 feet 6½ inches long and only 2 feet 8 inches wide! The sides were 3½ inches thick, and the bottom just over twice that thickness. With the keel, the canoe's backbone was just under 18 inches deep. Its inside height was 1 foot 9 inches.

I started laughing and Rory asked me why. 'I was just thinking,' I said, 'if we painted the bow bright red with "Long John Thomas" in big white letters. That would cause a bit of amusement in the Bristol Channel.'

'How fast do you think she'll go with Alex's Johnson 33?' Rory asked, after we'd both had a laugh.

'Depends how low she sits in the water. As a displacement craft she'll have a speed-length ratio of just over six knots. But if the bow is light enough to lift, we could double that speed. But don't forget we're having balsa trunks on each side for stability and they will really cut down our speed.'

At a little after eleven thirty, much to our relief, we heard voices. Onofre came into view through the bananas. But there were only four men with him, one of whom was his father. He carried a shotgun, the others carried machetes. 'Only five of you!' I exclaimed.

'The others are coming with Arturo. They would not come without him,' said Onofre. Arturo was the self-styled head of the village and Alex always referred to him as El Zorro – the fox – because of his cunning. I didn't like him at all. His eyes were much too shifty. The sort of person who, as we always said in the Army, would cut his grandmother's throat for tuppence.

149

A few minutes later he came marching into the clearing with twenty villagers behind him. They were all armed with shotguns and machetes. It occurred to me that an observer would instantly think they were going to war, not to pull a canoe to the water. I instinctively put my hand on the wad of 1,000-peso notes in my hip pocket and moved the sheath of the White Hunter round to cover the pocket. Rory eased himself off the rim of the canoe and came over to stand by my side.

'A fucking evil-looking bunch,' he said, quietly. 'They could kill us, take our money, bury us, and no one would ever know.'

Arturo strode over to me. 'Where is the Aguardiente?' he demanded, looking around as though he expected to see it hidden under a bush.

'It's at Maximino's house,' I said.

'But we need it now to give us strength. That is a very heavy canoe.'

'No!' Onofre interrupted before I could answer. 'It is better we pull the canoe first and drink afterwards. Come, let us cut poles to roll it on. Arturo, please fix the rope to the canoe.'

By being asked politely to do that, Arturo hadn't lost too much face when half the men went with Onofre.

Rory also went with them but I stayed behind. I was very interested to see how the still-grumbling Arturo was going to fix the rope. About eight hard-wood poles were cut from the cacao branches and trimmed to lengths of about one and a half inches longer than the inside width of the canoe. Both ends were then pointed and the poles were inserted at equal intervals inside the canoe, slanting across the width. The poles were then banged straight so that both points dug themselves into the softer wood of the canoe and held firmly.

A rope that Onofre had brought was tied securely to the pole nearest the stern, then wound round each of the other poles in turn, pulled tight and tied round the bow. The centre of my rope was slipped under the bow and the two ends brought over and tied to the first pole. The long ends were then laid out in a vee so that two rows of men could take hold of them and pull, the strain being placed evenly along the canoe by the poles, thus preventing the bow being torn off with the terrific strain.

By the time Arturo had finished supervising the rope, Onofre's party had cut thick saplings and laid them a few feet apart along the trail for the canoe to roll over, with the first one under the bow itself. Machetes and shotguns were placed in the bottom of the canoe and it looked like a small arsenal.

Positions were taken up on the ropes and several men ranged themselves along either side of the giant canoe. 'Pull!' commanded Onofre. Muscles tensed and fifty-six arms strained. Perhaps there were only fifty four pulling, for the canoe never budged and somebody called out that Arturo wasn't pulling! My heart dropped. We were never going to move it. But a determination seized everyone. Once more Onofre called 'Pull!' and the command was echoed by several others. To my relief, the canoe started to move. Cries of triumph went up and, at last, all the canoe was on the poles and it moved more easily. Behind where the poles started was a deep rut in the ground. When the poles terminated at the end of about a 100-foot run, everyone was sweating and exhausted. The poles that the canoe had traversed were carried to the front and the process repeated. I could see that it was going to take a long time. By the time we reached the coconut grove, everyone left the canoe and sat, panting, in the shade. To my astonishment, the villagers, with their ebony skins accustomed to the rays of the tropical sun, sought the shade of a small bush or even a tall clump of grass every time the poles had to be changed. More often than not, Onofre, Rory and I did the changing.

Arturo came up to me. 'My friend,' he said, 'fetch two bottles of Aguardiente here. The men need it. They will work much better with a mouthful or two of the liquor inside them.'

There was logic in that, I thought, and I told him to

send the weakest man off to Maximino's house. 'But only two bottles,' I said, sternly.

In the coconut grove, across the trail, ran a deep wide gully. Two big saplings were cut and laid over it, like a bridge, with the other poles across them. By the time this was ready, the man had returned with not two, but three, bottles. A cry went up and the bottles went the round of mouths. Onofre looked at me severely, but I just shrugged.

Aguardiente is pretty high proof and it doesn't take long to get to the brain cells. Muscles flexed, chests expanded and I reckoned that that lot could now pull a Sherman tank! To the accompaniment of war whoops, the canoe was on the move again.

By the time we reached the halfway mark, most of the men were half-pissed. I just hoped that the 'medicine' would last out.

'Are you sure you've done the right thing, Dad, giving them booze?' asked Rory.

'No, I'm not,' I said. 'But at least the canoe is moving and, if you notice, not all of them are drinking, just the piss-heads, and they seem to be the leaders. Keep *those* bastards happy and we're there.' To the men, I shouted: 'Come on, there's a crate waiting for you at Maximino's!' And off we went with renewed vigour.

The canoe went well across the flat marshland but we all decided to take a break before tackling the small hill, everyone sitting or lying in the shade. Rory came over and sat by me, his jeans soaked with sweat from the waist to the knees. 'Would you pull this fucking thing, on a Sunday afternoon, for a half a bottle of Aguardiente? I'm bloody sure I wouldn't,' he said.

'They all seem to be happy enough,' I said. 'And it's like half a bottle of Scotch to us. You play football for the Hop Pole on a Sunday afternoon for less than that. And they'll all have a good piss-up afterwards. And if they're happy, I'm happy. I just want to see this canoe sitting in the creek, then they can all get stuffed.'

The last dregs of the three bottles were drained, and Onofre got them all into motion once more. With ear-splitting whoops, they all grabbed the ropes or sides of the canoe. At the top of the rise, the most drunken ones collapsed, but the canoe was on a downward path, and they weren't needed. There were insufficient poles laid out to reach the bank, but the ground was soft and the adrenalin in the men was running as fast as the canoe. It shot over the bank and carried on sliding across the black mud. Then it stopped and sank, slightly, less than six feet from the nearest water of the receding tide.

'Well, Rory,' I said, with great satisfaction, 'there she is. All we've got to do now is wait six hours for the tide. What time do you make it?'

'Nearly four o'clock,' he said, to my surprise. 'Don't forget,' he continued, 'we didn't start pulling it until gone twelve thirty.'

'Three and a half hours, eh? I think they've earned their drink. Onofre!' He came over. 'How much do I owe you?'

'I worked eight days on the canoe,' he said, 'and another man helped me cut the trail; so that is 10,000 with 1,000 for him.'

'Right,' I said, 'here's the ten. Arturo!' I called. 'I'm giving Onofre another 3,000 pesos for you all to buy more Aguardiente – and thank you very much!'

'You joining us for celebration?' asked a very pleased Onofre. 'We kill two pigs tonight.'

'Yes,' I said. 'We'll come along later. Rory and I are going to cut some mangrove poles to strengthen the bottom of the canoe.'

After they had all gone, very content with their crate and extra 3,000 pesos, I handed Maximino a 1,000-peso note.

'Ho! What's this?' he exclaimed.

'For your cacao,' I said, 'and many thanks for your help.'

As Rory and I were cutting down two tall, very straight mangroves, he said: 'You realise, Dad, we've lost the bottle of whisky bet with Jerry?'

'Yeah!' I agreed. 'But I think we owe Jerry much more than a bottle of whisky.'

153

'I'll go along with that,' commented Rory, swinging the axe more vigorously.

It was dark when we finished eating a very nice meal of crab, rice, beans and banana, courtesy of Maximino's wife. The wind was blowing in our direction from the village and along the water course came the yells, shouts and laughter of much merry-making.

'Listen to them,' said Maximino, sitting down on the second floor with his legs dangling over the side.

'Are you going to join them?' I asked, sitting down next to him.

'No,' he replied, solemnly. 'I am not of their village, and they might kill me in their fun. I would advise that you and your son do not join them either.'

'I have no intention of doing so,' I said. 'I'm quite content to wait here. Will you take Onofre's rope back tomorrow?'

'No,' he said. 'He will come here for it when he wants it.'

'What do you think of the canoe?'

Maximino sucked a piece of crab from his scant and yellow teeth. 'It is good, but ceibo is bad wood. It will split after a few months.'

'But I am going to nail metal bands round it, and put on two coats of paint.'

'That is very good. It should get you to England. With paint and metal bands it would last a long time in these quiet waters and it would make a very good cargo boat. It could carry many, many tons of bananas. And one thing is for sure: it will never sink. But in the sea, the pounding of the waves is much different. You must put ribs inside it.'

'We're going to,' I said. 'We've bought some really good timber and the ribs will be bolted, not nailed.'

Rory sat himself next to me. 'What time do you make it?' I asked him.

'You asked me that quarter of an hour ago. Just turned quarter past seven.'

154

I looked up at the sky. There was no moon, and clouds hid many of the stars. Where the creek started was a black hole. There was no sign of any water coming through.

'What time do you think the tide will be here?' I asked Maximino.

'We will see the water very soon now,' he said. 'I think you will be able to leave at nine o'clock. The water comes in very fast.'

'It's going to be pretty eerie going back without a moon,' said Rory.

'Yes,' I agreed. 'But at high tide we won't have to worry about the sandbanks. We'll just keep mid-stream.'

'Maximino?' queried Rory.

'Señor!'

'Are you sure that little engine of ours will be strong enough to tow that canoe?'

'Yes,' he said, 'but don't try to go too fast. You'll make it all right. I think the clouds will clear soon and there will be more starlight. You have sheerpins and tools?'

'Yes,' I said, 'but I doubt if we'll hit anything with the tide high, and I put a new pin in the propeller last night.'

The canoe was startling white against the black surroundings and looked absolutely gigantic in the small creek. It had settled quite deeply in the mud on its side and keel and I hoped the buoyancy was sufficient to right it before water poured over the rim.

It was like waiting for a kettle to boil as we sat there, straining our eyes for the first sign of water. In my impatience I wanted to walk across the black mud and take out the short poles and Onofre's rope, but the mosquitoes and sand-flies were out in droves and immediately started eating anyone who set foot on the bank.

For the umpteenth time, Rory echoed my worse fear that the canoe wouldn't float at all! Maximino laughed. 'It will float, all right,' he said. 'Have no fear.'

For me, it was very similar – but also different – to the times I had waited for each of my sons to be born. Would the baby be deformed or not function properly in some part? After all, the canoe had been carved on dry land

155

with little measuring, with only the eye to make sure it was symmetrical. Perhaps, if it did float, it would sit in the water at a slant, or one end would be lower in the water than the other. Those were reasonable enough fears, I thought, when one considered the mathematics employed to build a hull of that size.

The yells coming down the creek seemed to be a few decibels higher, and some were quite blood-curdling. I felt a bit like the guilty whites who sold firewater to the Red Indians in the days of the old Wild West.

'I hope the buggers don't come swarming down here in their canoes with the tide to see why we insulted them by not joining them,' said Rory, uneasily. 'Where *is* that fucking water?'

It was a little before a quarter to eight when Maximino suddenly said: 'Look!' Sure enough, the water was showing itself in the form of a very broad, shiny black serpent, slithering quite fast across the mud. It divided into several heads, forging along the lowest parts, one making straight for the canoe. Such a strange tingle of excitement manifested itself in my stomach as the first water licked the canoe, as though baptising it. Soon the water was all around it.

'It won't be long now, Dad,' said Rory, with obviously the same excitement within him as I had. 'If we had made the afternoon tide, we could have taken some really good photos of it in the water for the first time.'

'No we couldn't,' I told him, getting to my feet. 'I haven't any film left. Give me a cigarette. Now that the water's here, the insects won't be so bad. I'm going to punt Arthur's canoe across to have a look at her.'

'It will be another hour yet, Dad,' protested Rory.

'I know, but I just feel like doing something. You stay here. I can manage OK.'

I was wrong about the insects. I had to slap my hands and face while I frantically untied the rope on Arthur's canoe. But as soon as I was afloat, the insects left me. I imagined I was a pilot going out to a destroyer. Certainly, Arthur's canoe was diminutive against the long white shape. With pride, I went all round her, and to my joy I saw that she was beginning to right herself. My oar caught a part of my rope which had been dropped on the canoe's downward run, and most of it was embedded in the mud under the weight. I went round again to the side opposite the list. 'Permission to come aboard,' I said. And I clambered over the side. The canoe never budged under my weight. Exultation surged within me as I started to undo Onofre's rope. Next, I knocked out the short poles with the heel of my palm. There was a sucking noise, and she righted herself completely. I tried pulling my rope but the canoe was still resting on it. I sat on the rim, finishing my cigarette. Waiting.

Minutes later, Rory and Maximino came wading through the knee-deep water, pulling up each foot with effort from the mud. Maximino was carrying a long oar.

I got out, and the two of them put their shoulders against the stern. I quickly lent a hand. 'She's going, Dad,' puffed Rory. She was, too. The mud suddenly released her and she was floating, upright as a die and moving effortlessly. 'Just look at her, Dad,' Rory gushed. 'She's absolutely beautiful.'

Maximino put the oar inside, jumped up and wriggled himself over the rim. He quickly untied my rope, pulled it out of the water and threw it into the bottom. 'I will push her through the first two, very sharp bends,' he said, using the oar as a punt. 'You bring my canoe for me to come back in.'

It only seemed a few seconds before he and the canoe had disappeared into the darkness. 'She moves so easily!' Rory exclaimed.

But, of course, the obstinate old Yamaha 15 refused to start. For ages Rory and I took turns at pulling the starter cord. Finally, she fired, and I gave her a few hard revs to warm her up and clean the shit out of her. Then with Rory holding the rope of Maximino's canoe we chugged, slowly, into the darkness. Despite the high, overhead branches, forming a canopy, we could see quite well when our eyes became accustomed.

'I think Maximino is probably in Tumaco,' Rory commented, for bend after bend there was no sign of him. We caught him up where the creek broadened and not far from the main channel.

Maximino told me to go alongside in a central position so that the big canoe protruded fore and aft. He had replaced the first and last of the hardwood poles and one end of my rope was tied to the one in the bow. While I kept the Yamaha ticking over, Maximino told Rory to tie the shorter end of the rope to the bow of Arthur's canoe. Then he wrapped the rope all down the side of the big canoe, round the stern, up to the second hardwood pole and secured it very tight on the engine mount.

'Hey, Maximino,' Rory told him, 'that's stupid – much better to have the bows of both canoes level.'

Maximino became instantly enraged. 'Never let a gringo tell a black man what to do,' he stormed, 'especially in the jungle and in a canoe.'

'Don't answer back, Rory,' I said, in English before he could speak. 'Maximino knows what he's doing.'

Maximino's anger subsided as fast as it had risen. Before getting into his canoe, he shook our hands. 'Good luck,' he said. 'Don't open the throttle more than halfway. You'll make pretty good time.'

As the darkness swallowed him I thought how incredible was that underlying feeling of the black and white complex. Here was a man who had befriended us and had been an easily chatting amigo, and we had shared good conversation at his own dinner table. But the way he had spat out the word 'gringo', and the belligerence and indignation in his tone could only mean that all the time, he really resented us.

I could sense that Rory was still bristling, but thought it best to say nothing about it. 'Right, me old darling,' I said. 'Sit yourself down in the bow and let your old Dad get you home safely.'

With the way the two canoes glided easily through the water, the throttle only a little way open, Rory quickly forgot his grievance. As we entered the broader channel,

158

the noise of revelry from the village grew louder; it was now accompanied by dance music and we could see the red glow of a bonfire in the sky.

I brought the canoes round on a wide turn and gradually opened the throttle when we were in mid-stream. We were going quite fast. I could tell by the movements of Rory's head that he was singing, and I was grateful for the noise of the engine – he has a tone-deaf voice like a ruptured frog!

Maximino was right about the clouds clearing, and there were many stars. Even so, as Rory had forecast, it was very eerie. In the dark, there is little perspective; the islands appeared as one continuous black blob and seemed much closer to us than they really were. Also, there was no recognisable feature. I just hoped we wouldn't lose our way. Another thing I had experienced about islands in the dark is that a smaller island in front of a larger one cannot be seen as such – it just sits in dead ground to the eyes.

Rory suddenly began gesturing for me to turn right, so I did so, wondering what all the fuss was about. Then we were both ducking to avoid the overhanging branches of the small island where the very wide channel started. For a moment I was completely disorientated so headed straight out to the middle of the channel, which was about a mile wide, and, sure enough, after ten minutes or so, we saw the flash of the far-off beacon. I relaxed again. We were all right now. The engine, too, was running sweetly. Every now and then, Rory stretched out his hand to touch the big canoe, each time turning towards me afterwards with the thumbs-up sign.

My thoughts returned to Maximino and I wondered whether an inferiority complex were the reason for black men's aggression – or, at least, one of the reasons. When I was working as a casual sub-editor on the *Western Mail* in Perth, Western Australia, I'd noticed that many Australians always seemed as if they needed to prove something all the time. I had seen this same trait in their soldiers in Korea. I discussed it with an Australian journalist on one occasion. 'We're pretty remote from the rest of the world,' he said, 'and with everything happening in Britain, Europe and America we sometimes feel a bit left behind. You pommy bastards are always up to new tricks. And then we have to try to catch up.'

'You mean you feel a bit inferior?' I asked.

'You could call it that. The reason you couldn't get a job on a Sydney newspaper was because the editor knew you were ex-Fleet Street and were therefore better than he was, and you might pinch his job. In Perth, here, the pace isn't quite that competitive.'

'I shouldn't worry too much about your inferiority complex,' I told him, good-humouredly. 'You ex-cons *are* inferior!' He'd responded, equally good-humouredly, that it was my turn to buy the round.

Mid-way along the wide channel, Rory stood up quickly and peered into the big canoe. Then he came running back to me, holding on to the sides because the sea had become a bit choppy. I throttled back. 'Water's coming into our boat!' he said. I handed him one of the half-coconut shells. 'It's probably that soft core in the bow,' I told him. 'Go and have a look.'

He stepped over into the big canoe and walked to the front. He began bailing. After several minutes he returned and reported that it was the soft core, but it was only a small trickle. I told him to stay in the big canoe and keep watch.

When we reached the main channel which formed Tumaco's harbour, the chop changed to small, sweeping waves, like a tiny swell. While Arthur's canoe began bucking, the big canoe just cut through them without a judder. The electricity was back on in Tumaco and I headed straight for the island's shoreline. 'What's the time?' I called to Rory. 'Six minutes past midnight,' he shouted back. For more than three hours I had been holding the steering handle and throttle, and though I had changed hands periodically, my fingers were stiff with cramp. I called Rory to me. 'You can have a go,' I said, 'to give my hands a break. Keep the nose pointed to the lights. You'll find that you've got to steer to the left all the time because that big bitch wants to pull us to the right.'

Rory soon got used to it, and I went to inspect the leak in the big canoe. The water was coming in quite fast so I started bailing to put some life back into my hands. That core would definitely need reinforcing with other timber as well as tar, and that might well mean a half-day's work out of our precious time.

Close in to the shoreline where the water showed hardly a ripple I signalled for Rory to turn, and we followed the waterfront to the bridge. Several men were working with floodlights in the coconut factory, the fish market and petrol station. All stopped what they were doing and stared with surprise as we went past. I wondered what they thought of that long white shape.

Rory asked me to steer through the bridge. The outgoing tide was running with us and carried us through with no problem at all. The three houses in our little bay were all in darkness. Obviously, Redmond and Yeannie had thought we were staying the night at Maximino's. The doors were locked so I rapped on our bedroom window and called softly to Yeannie. Immediately the light went on and she opened the wooden shutter.

She was overjoyed to see me. 'I've been lying awake, wondering where you were,' she said, kissing me.

'Never mind about that,' snorted Rory. 'Open the door!'

Redmond came staggering out of his bedroom with his sheet wrapped round him. 'Have you got it?' he asked, only a long yawn suppressing excitement.

'Yep,' said Rory. 'Come and have a look at her.'

Yeannie had also draped herself in a sheet, and the four of us went down to the beach, Rory jabbering to Redmond about the journey and day's events.

'Huy!' exclaimed Yeannie, when she saw the sleek white shape on the black water. 'It's as long as our bay!'

'Look how small Arthur's canoe is alongside it!' added Redmond.

'One thing's for sure,' I told them, 'we'll never be able to haul it up on to dry land. There were twenty-eight of us

161

pulling it to the creek. We'll have to work on her where she is.'

'Then how are we going to paint underneath?' asked Redmond.

'Simple,' I said. 'We'll turn her over, do the bottom and turn her back again. Paint will soon dry in this heat.'

Mid-morning, when Alex saw the canoe, he gave a long, low whistle. 'I think I'll get myself one like that,' he said with envy.

I asked him about the Johnson 33. 'A problem,' he said. 'Can you come with me to the repair shop?'

The Johnson 33 was sixties vintage; but engines were well-built in those days and gave more power for less petrol. This particular engine, however, had two vital parts missing – the petrol pump and carburettor. It had been in the repair shop for more than a year, and I think the man had probably sold the parts, thinking that Alex was never going to pay for the repairs. Also, the bill was 22,000 pesos, not 9,000 as Alex had informed me. The parts would cost another 20,000, but £280 was cheap for an engine considering that a new one cost £2,000.

The really bad news was that the parts would take about two months to arrive. Because the engine was so old, the concessionaire in Cali would have to send to the US for them. The only other engines the man had for sale were at least £1,000 second-hand.

Despondent, I went with Alex to two other places which had outboards for sale. But the prices were much higher than I could afford to pay without waiting for more money to arrive from England.

I called in to see Jerry. 'The only engine I can legitimately sell you is the Yamaha 15,' he said. 'I could write that off for 25,000 pesos.'

I reasoned that the Yamaha had pushed two canoes through the water without effort at three miles an hour; and I wanted an engine only for use in harbours and emergency.

'OK,' I said. 'It's a deal.'

162

'Do you think you'll be ready to leave by the 9th?' he asked.

'I sincerely hope so.'

'Well, I want to give you people a farewell dinner. Shall we say seven-thirty, my place, on the 8th?'

'Lovely,' I said, with obvious delight. 'Thank you very much. Any chance of a steak?'

'My pleasure,' he said. 'But I'll be calling round to see how you're getting on before that.'

The boys and Yeannie were also disappointed about the Johnson 33, but very pleased about the dinner invite. We hadn't eaten beefsteak since we left the *Buccaneer*.

14

That afternoon, we started work with a vengeance. Redmond sharpened the two saws lent by Alex and Jerry while Rory and I designed on paper the shape of the sides and height of deck. A bone of contention was the latter. Rory and Redmond had no wish to be cramped with a low ceiling in the living accommodation for ninety days, the estimated duration of the voyage. I told them they would have to put up with it or the centre of gravity would be too high. In the end they gave in. Even so, a six-foot headroom was a colossal height for such a narrow beam, but, I reasoned, the two balsa trunks on either side would compensate for this.

A lawyer friend of Alex was staying with him, and the two of them helped to turn the canoe over with the aid of a double-pulley arrangement anchored to a tree.

First, we trimmed the keel to a width of three inches. I had asked Onofre to make it six inches wide to allow for damage and scoring when the canoe was hauled to the creek. By the end of three days, the bottom had been smoothed, tarred, painted with anti-corrosive paint and strengthened with metal bands at four-foot intervals. On the fourth day we painted all the underside white.

At high tide we worked chest-high in the water. When the tide went out, the beach on which the canoe lay was dry. Late afternoon on the fourth day, when the canoe was afloat, Alex, his friend and the four of us ranged ourselves along the side to turn it the right way up. On the third attempt at rocking it, the canoe went over – and floated with water inside it almost up to the brim! We all clambered aboard. Full of water and carrying six of us it still floated.

'Maximino was right,' I said, happy as a sandboy, 'it will never sink!'

With buckets and saucepans we bailed out the water. Jerry arrived just as we were finishing. 'Now that,' he commented, 'is some canoe.' I decided it was time to splice the mainbrace – and out came the bottle of rum.

Over the next four days we measured, cut and shaped the ribs, and built the sides with planks, clinker style. Jerry called to see us again on the 7th, and his immediate comment was that the sides were too high.

'You've got to reduce them by at least eighteen inches, no matter what Rory and Redmond say, or you'll be top heavy.'

'That's what I think,' I agreed. 'Also, we've another problem – the canoe is sitting lower with the weight of the timber and water is not only coming in through the core in the bow but through the stern as well. We'll have to put on more tar.'

'Better still,' said Jerry, 'why not cut off the back end completely and insert a new piece of wood?'

'I know that's a good idea,' I said, 'but we just haven't got the time. What I intend to do is get out of Tumaco with all materials and tools, so that we conform to regulations, and call in at the first bit of secluded beach and finish building her.'

With the additional work of reducing the height and scaling and re-sealing the stern and bow with tar, by the end of the next day we still had the balsa trunks to put on, the rudder to be built, the deck to be laid and the mast of very slender mangrove to be erected ready for Yeannie's sail of twenty flour sacks which she had double-sewn with very strong thread. There was also an engine mount to be built outside the housing for the rudder, for no way would the U-clamps of the Yamaha fit over the wide back.

'It's no good,' I said, 'we'll have to ask DAS for more time, and pay the extra money. We must have the balsa trunks and engine in position before we leave; and some decking in place to keep things dry. Rory and I will carry on working tomorrow while you, Redmond, and Yeannie go to DAS. Yeannie – tell them a real hard-luck story. Five days will be sufficient.'

That evening we all went in Arthur's canoe to Jerry's house for the dinner send-off, even though we knew we wouldn't be leaving the next day. After drinking several rum and cokes, and seeing the size of the juicy steaks on the table, and the bottles of wine to wash them down, we soon forgot the troubles with the canoe.

It is always surprising how visitors never really get to know a person or fully appreciate a friendship until it is time to leave. I felt sad that I would be saying goodbye to Jerry. Over dinner he told us a personal confidence: Carlitos was not his real son, but adopted; and Jerry had now obtained Canadian citizenship for him.

'Well, that's one little black boy who's going to have a good start in the civilised world,' I commented. We also discovered the reason for Jerry's tinged Canadian accent: he was born in Holland and went to Canada when he was very young. He could now speak three languages: Dutch, English and Spanish.

After dinner, Jerry brought out another bottle of rum which he and Rory started to drink. The rest of us continued with the wine.

'So, you've had no trouble at all with your negro neighbour,' Jerry said. 'Probably that's because you've never given *him* any trouble.'

'Precisely,' I rejoined. 'I still wonder about the true situation between him and the Benitezes. In fact, the last time there was any gunfire was on the night when he'd set fire to the grass. We've got ourselves a shotgun, by the way. Alex's 16-bore. Rory swapped the air rifle for it. Alex has really got a good bargain. That air rifle cost £116.'

'And you've had no night prowlers interested in the canoe?'

'Yes. About a couple of nights ago. The dogs that Alex has started barking. We got up to have a look. The lights were back on again, and there were two men in a canoe, just sitting off-shore. Rory and I went down the beach, flashing the shotgun, and after about half an hour, they left. The tide was on the way out, and once that bitch is grounded no one is going to move her without a winch or a crane. And the two men paddled off. But in the day-time, Jerry – loads of people come in close to have a look at her. She really is eye-catching.'

'I reckon she looks more like an MTB than a canoe,' said Redmond.

'Oh, there's one thing I've always forgotten to mention,' said Jerry. 'What was the name of that island you were on in the Galapagos?'

'Isabela,' I said. 'Why?'

'That was the name! In March, I think it was, or possibly February – I only read the report in the paper briefly – the island caught fire.'

'What?' we all asked, aghast. 'Are you sure?'

He nodded. 'Positive. The people had to be taken off. They lived in the south, right? Nearly all the animals were burnt to death. Ecuador created a big stink because it took a long time before anyone went to their aid.'

'How terrible!' said Yeannie. 'And no one was killed?'

'I don't think so – just the animals.'

'What caused the fire?' I asked. 'A volcano?'

'I think the report said it was hot lava from the small volcano.'

'That was the one next to ours,' said Rory.

'I always felt uneasy there,' added Redmond.

'I think everyone did, deep down,' I said. 'It was like the saying: Living on the edge of a volcano.'

We all wondered what had happened to Oscar and Negra.

'There you are,' I observed. 'It was a good job Yeannie was illegal or we'd all have been running for our lives.'

'We'd probably be dead,' said Rory. 'We were higher up the volcano than all the other people!'

'All those donkeys and cattle,' said Yeannie, sadly.

After many such comments and expressions of sadness about the animals, Jerry asked Yeannie if she had found the islands to be romantic.

She reached her hand across the table and placed it on

167

mine. She laughed. 'Gerald and I fell in love there,' she said. 'But, no. It is the voyage – the atmosphere on the ship that is romantic. On the islands themselves there is too much control – essential control – for romanticism. But in a secluded part, or better on a small, uninhabited island, without the influence and knowledge of the control – well, yes, it could be romantic. Don't forget, though, that there is much virgin lava, especially near the sea, and I don't find lava at all romantic.' She laughed again. 'And there is a lot of bird-shit on the small islands. In fact, they stink just like a zoo. As Gerald always said, they are not a person's idea of the desert isle.'

It was well after midnight before we finished talking and drinking. And outside it was as black as pitch. To make matters worse, while we'd been bathed in bright lights from electricity supplied by Plan's own private generator, the lights of Tumaco were out. We groped our way to where the canoe was moored to Plan's private wharf, the water looking like ink.

I got in first and was busying myself, feeling for the controls of the engine, when there was a thud and a yell from Rory. 'Dad! Dad!' he cried, giggling. 'Look. My arse is in the water!' He had fallen over the side of the canoe and was hanging with both hands and the inside of his knees.

'Get him up, you two,' I said, with desultoriness, for I was almost as pissed as he was. They dragged him in, and he sat in the bottom in the water, trying to sing.

'Redmond,' I called, endeavouring to keep my balance, 'give me a hand to start this fucking thing.'

'Are you sure you are going to be able to steer?' asked Redmond, when the engine was chugging away.

'Of course I bloody well am. I could steer this bloody thing blindfolded. That was a beautiful meal, wasn't it?'

'The steak was absolutely delicious,' Yeannie shouted over the noise of the engine.

'All aboard the Skylark!' I commanded. 'Batten all

168

watertight doors! Action stations! Periscope up! Cast off, for'ard!' And away we went.

No way could I see the bridge; and all the shoreline looked the same. I just kept the canoe pointed in the general direction.

'You've missed the bridge, Dad!' Redmond suddenly shouted. Yeannie was yelling the same. The next thing I knew we had hit the bank, and the three of us ended up in the bottom of the canoe with Rory!

And I don't remember a thing after that until I woke the next morning. Redmond and Yeannie steered the canoe under the bridge and got us home. And Rory got into bed with his wet clothes and boots on!

15

Rory and I had just finished securing the four balsa trunks to the sides when Yeannie and Redmond returned from DAS in Arthur's canoe at 1 p.m. the following day. Considering we both had hangovers, I thought we had worked extremely well.

'Gerald, we have very serious news,' said Yeannie. 'We are all illegal here – and we may be deported.'

Alarm clutched me, for I could see that she wasn't joking. 'What do you mean, deported?' I answered, angrily. 'And who said we are illegal?'

'We are!' insisted Redmond. 'Our time was up yesterday, the 8th.'

'Don't be silly,' I said, irritably. 'How can it have been? We arrived in Colombia on the 8th of February. Count ninety days from then, and you can't get away from the fact that it's the 9th of May. We've counted it enough times in Yeannie's diary and on the calendar.'

'Yes, but we've all made a mistake,' said Redmond. 'You don't count *from* the 8th, but include that first day in the count.'

'Aw, shit!' I said, absolutely exasperated. 'Do you really? So what happens now? I hope you explained the genuine mistake.'

'We did,' said Yeannie, 'but we all have to be at DAS as soon as possible tomorrow morning with our passports and two small photographs of each of us. We also have to have our fingerprints taken.'

'Where the devil are we going to get photographs from?' I wanted to know.

Redmond replied that they had been to see Jerry and he had arranged for us to be at Plan's photographic department at eight the next morning. 'It will only take a couple of hours for developing and printing,' he added.

'Good boy,' I said. 'How serious is the situation?'

'They've got a new chief there. Not the same one that we saw beforehand. He said we have to pay 20,000 pesos plus stamp duty, but I think he fancies Yeannie so she may be able to talk him into letting us go a bit cheaper. But there's a bitch of a secretary there, and she wants us deported.'

'I hope we don't have to pay 20,000 pesos,' I said. 'That's more than £120.'

'And bang goes our piss-up in Miami,' grumbled Rory.

An hour later, Alex delivered more disturbing news. The port captain was a little angry that we had not been back to see him. He'd requested that we attend his office immediately. After a quick bite to eat, Yeannie and I left in Arthur's canoe. I told the two boys to start on the deck.

Yeannie quickly pacified Capitán Gutierrez with an explanation about the sequence of events from wanting to build a motor yacht to actually building a dug-out canoe. Many times she stressed that we'd had no intention of being rude; it was simply that we had been working very hard and had been preoccupied.

Capitán Gutierrez replied that he quite understood. He smiled. 'But again you have called on me when I have to go away,' he said. 'However, my PA will see to your needs. He will inspect your boat tomorrow and if everything is satisfactory, he will issue the necessary documents. Perhaps you could call for him in your canoe as he has no transport.'

'Certainly,' said Yeannie, 'but it won't be until the afternoon.' And she quickly told him about the problem with DAS.

'I think you will be all right,' he said. 'And I wish you a very safe voyage.'

Capitán Gutierrez's surmise proved true next morning: we were all right with DAS – but it had been touch and go. 'Deport them! Deport them!' the secretary urged. But the chief told her, curtly, to shut up and he took Yeannie off to his private office. There Yeannie found out he hated the blacks, and, if he had his way, he would shoot the lot of them!

She returned, all smiles, and informed us that we had to pay only 10,000 pesos plus stamp duty which was a mere 16 pesos for the four of us.

'We have until the 15th to leave Tumaco,' she said. 'Then we'll be issued with a *salvoconducto* which will allow us ten days to be out of Colombian waters.'

'Marvellous!' I said, and I thanked the chief very much. After we'd had our fingerprints taken, he told us to come back on the 15th when our *salvoconductos* would be ready. We didn't have to pay anything until then.

On the way back I asked Yeannie how many kisses she'd had to give the chief. She laughed. 'None,' she said, 'but he did invite me to have lunch with him! Most of the time he was talking about the negro problem, and I told him about my father's work in Chile. The chief is a very nice man – a gentleman. He said the negro problem in Tumaco is very serious indeed. The police are always arresting them for robbing and killing. Our position here is very dangerous, Gerald. The sooner we leave, the better. Vandalism is terrible; and every day, the police have to be harder with the negroes because they are now attacking the police. But the problem is really the poverty and social conditions.'

'I don't envy him his job,' I said, 'and he certainly sounds a gentleman. It was a good thing that woman wasn't in charge. Did you see the dirty looks she gave us?'

We called in at Plan and I gave Jerry a cheque for life-jackets and an iron anchor. I also bought his camera. With the small ship's compass I possessed we now had all the regulation equipment for a canoe. After telling us, to our relief, that he thought our canoe was good, the port captain's PA said we would probably have to buy a radio in Panama to satisfy the authorities there. 'And for 2,000 pesos I can let you have charts of the waters up to Panama,' he added.

Even with the extra six days we had still not positioned the mast when the time came for departure. The back end had given us a lot of trouble and we'd had to reinforce it considerably as well as build a mount for the engine. The deck, too, presented many problems with having to curve the outside boards to the shape of the sides. Then each plank had to be caulked with coconut fibre and tar, a most lengthy and laborious task.

On the morning of the 15th, after we'd collected our *salvoconductos* from DAS and the necessary documents from the port captain's office, we had to wait for the tide. Suddenly, five nuns, looking like giant penguins, came down the beach, and, to my complete surprise, started blessing the boat. They made quite a ceremony of it, too. Hugo had invited them to do so and he handed Yeannie a large crucifix. With more realism, he gave me a half-bottle of whisky! 'We will all be praying for you tonight,' he said, putting the wind up Yeannie completely. What with the nuns' blessing, the crucifix and Hugo's words she felt sure we were all going to die.

To make light of the situation, I told her: 'With the nuns' blessing and the weight of that crucifix on board, the boat's bound to sink.' She didn't think it was at all funny. In fact, she said that *El Señor* would be furious with me.

I had spent a whole day servicing the engine and putting fresh oil in the gearbox. I had asked at several places for a new choke lever but without success. Not a pleasing prospect was the knowledge that the engine lid had to be removed to start the engine, even when hot. There was obviously something not quite right inside the engine for this to be necessary, probably faulty reed valves, for a hot engine never needs choking to start it.

Alex arrived from the jungle with the tide, bearing bananas and oranges. Jerry and Arthur also came to see us off. 'If you get into any trouble up the coast, and if there's a phone handy, well – you know the number. I'm off to Cali on tomorrow's early morning plane, but you can always get a message to me.' He and Arthur shook us

173

all warmly by the hand. 'Don't forget to write when you get to England – and don't forget I want a copy of the book,' Jerry added.

As we couldn't go the regular way to the shipping channel – the water wasn't yet high enough under the bridge – Alex and his lawyer friend suggested that they guided us out past the uninhabited island.

'But no boats go that way,' I exclaimed. 'I've heard it's the worst part.'

Alex shrugged. 'If you want to leave now, there's no other choice, unless you wait two more hours for the tide, or stay here another night and leave on the early morning tide. But I can get you through all right. I know the way.'

The boys and Yeannie were eager to leave, and so was I. We had said our goodbyes and everything was loaded, ready. Also, if we waited until we could pass under the bridge we would probably still be in the turbulence out there when it was dark.

We had plenty of food on board, seventeen gallons of fresh water and twenty-two gallons of petrol. As we crossed the calm water over to the uninhabited island, I estimated our speed was about four knots. We were all very happy and excited that at last, we had built our boat, everything about it and about us was legal, and we were on our way to England.

Every so often, Alex stopped and tested the depth with an oar.

We could see the big waves rolling in, frothy white arcing and curling as they grounded, then breaking fiercely on the island's shore. To my satisfaction, the canoe rammed its way through them with hardly a judder, while Alex's dinghy was tossed on high. In minor celebration, I took a slug of whisky.

Rory, Redmond and Yeannie had been standing on deck, waving to the small group growing ever smaller on the Benitezes' beach but they quickly got down into the canoe as the waves became higher and higher. About a mile or so out, Alex turned his dinghy and came back to us. One minute, he was below us, the next, above us. 'I daren't go any further,' he shouted. 'You've got to get to that channel buoy. Can you see it?'

'Yes!' I shouted back.

'When you reach it, head straight in for the shore, and camp there until tomorrow morning. Good luck, all of you.'

Just before he allowed the dinghy to be swept away from us with the next wave, I saw that his and his friend's faces were very grim. I took another shot of whisky. The marker buoy, whenever a wave soared us high enough to see it, looked like a needle sticking up on the horizon.

One thing everybody had been right about – the waves off Tumaco's shores were colossal even in the deep-water channel, and we were about five miles from it. Between was a sea that had gone completely berserk. It wasn't long before Redmond threw up over the side. The waves were now coming at us from two directions, a true sign of great turbulence. It was easy to see why Alex had turned back. His little dinghy wouldn't have stood a chance.

I told Rory to take over the engine so that I could see better. I also told Redmond to lie face down on the deck and hold on tight. Yeannie's face was as white as a sheet. She sat, nursing her beloved coffee plant.

Two miles further on and the waves were higher and hitting us more rapidly. But the canoe was taking it all right, even though the terrific force of the water smacking the sides was sending jets of water through the clinker joins. But I knew that when the dry timber swelled with the wet, the planks would fit tighter together.

I estimated we were only a mile from the marker buoy when we entered the worst part, the sea raging at us from all angles. I saw one tremendous wave building up fast on the right and I yelled to Rory to bring her round to meet it. But too late: the giant wave hit us broadside on, heeling the canoe so that the side of the deck touched the water before the balsas righted us again. But not before the very-ill Redmond, the mast, a box of food, timber and other things had been shot overboard.

'Bring her round hard to get Redmond!' I screamed,

175

sick with fear in my stomach that a big shark might be lurking. Yeannie grabbed a life-jacket and threw it to Redmond as soon as he surfaced. He looked so alone and pathetically small in that broiling sea. One moment he was out of sight with a wave pouring over him, the next he was on top of a wave and higher than we were. But I could see he was quite calm and swimming with slow, powerful strokes, pushing floating timber out of his way and collecting the life-jacket. I knew it was going to be quite a job to get him back on board, and I began praying to God, anybody or anything.

It was then that the propeller struck a piece of wood, snapping the sheerpin instantly. We were without propulsion! But Redmond was now right close in near the stern. I leaned over the side, reaching for him. He grabbed my arm as the sea sank away beneath, and there he hung, smiling at me, until the next wave lifted him and I was able to pull him so that he pitched head-first into the boat.

'How do you feel, mate?' I asked him, relief coursing through me.

'I think I'll live,' he responded. 'But we're in the shit again, aren't we, Dad?'

'No we're not,' I told him. 'She'll take a lot more pounding than this.' We had two oars on board. I handed him one. 'We've got to keep the waves off the arse-end while Rory gets the engine up and puts in a new sheerpin.'

'But the bastard things are coming at us from all directions,' he said.

'Yes, I know. But the biggest buggers are coming from the right. They're the ones we've got to worry about.'

'Where are the tools?' Rory shouted.

'In the yellow plastic container!' I called back, squeezing salt water from my moustache and beard.

'Oh, my Christ!' exclaimed Redmond. 'That was next to the food box on deck!' We looked. The deck was completely bare. There was no possible way we could remove the engine. The clamp bolts were very old and could only be turned with a shifting spanner. The only tool we had left was a plug spanner which I had fortunately

176

put in my jeans pocket and forgotten about after giving the plugs a final clean and sandpapering just before leaving.

'Rory,' I said, with a calmness I didn't feel, 'can you put in a new sheerpin with the engine tilted? Redmond and I will try to keep her head-on to the biggest waves with the oars.'

'I'll try,' he said. I really had to hand it to him. He had to lie on his belly, with the inside of his feet curled round a cross-member to stop him going overboard, and each wave rolling over his head and arms. At the same time he had to hammer out, with the plug spanner, the split-pin securing the propeller nut, take the nut and propeller off, insert a new sheerpin and reassemble.

Though Redmond and I strove with the oars, the big canoe wouldn't budge from the way she wanted to float – broadside-on to the biggest waves which cascaded towards us like a long mountain ridge flecked with white, smaller waves on their high slopes from trough to top. At the same time, ranges of hills were rushing towards us from the front, back and other side. It was as though we were in a giant's bath-tub, and he was swirling the water every which way with his hand. But the mountain range on the right always hit us first, tipping us over to the crazy angle where the top of the boat touched the water.

'Oh, my guts are killing me,' groaned Redmond. 'I can't do any more, Dad. I really can't.' He sat down in the bottom of the canoe, eyes closed, and clutching his stomach. Yeannie picked up the oar.

'You sit in the bottom with Redmond!' I ordered her. 'Look after him and the coffee plant. Remember! That's got to go to England! And I don't want you going overboard as well.'

'Darling, I'm so very frightened,' she cried, almost in tears.

'Don't be,' I said to her, softly, putting an arm around her. 'We're all right. Honestly. I know the sea. This canoe is good. We're all right.'

She looked so white-faced and afraid as she sat down next to Redmond that my heart almost burst with love for

177

her. She was a very brave woman. True bravery, as we always maintained in Korea, was when a person was afraid to do something, but did it. It was always *empty* beer bottles that a so-called hero threw at a machine-gun nest – never full ones! Yeannie had been very afraid to get on board in the first place. I thought how absurd it was that the boys had doubted her love for me.

I was determined that this belligerent, cruel Colombian sea wasn't going to harm her.

'How are you going, Rory?' I asked him.

'All right,' he spluttered. 'Nearly finished.'

'Good boy,' I said.

As I once more put the whisky bottle to my lips, my thoughts turned to Jim Bouston, who lived in Bromyard. We had become good drinking companions, and I always considered him to be a true hero. Just before the end of World War II he had stepped on a mine in Germany. He now had an artificial leg. For our send-off from Bromyard, Pete and Annie Robinson had organised an underwear party at the Hop Pole. Into the midst of the shimmering cami-knickers, suspenders, stockings and the duller tone of men's underpants, had walked Jim, the harness of his artificial leg visible on his naked thigh.

'Sod what they think,' he had said to me. 'It's an underwear party, and I'm in my underwear.' Later, he handed me a wooden-handled clasp knife. 'I'm not giving it to you, or selling it to you; I'm a bit superstitious about knives. I'm just letting you have it. I've had it for a long, long time. So look after it. And look after yourselves as well. When you get back, I want the knife back.'

'Finished!' said Rory. 'Ooh! I've got cramp in my big toe!'

'Never mind about that,' I said. 'Let's get the engine going and get some sort of control over this boat.'

'Whew, Dad!' he said. 'You've not been drinking whisky!'

'Just a swig or two. Some fucker's always got to be happy in times of woe to keep up the morale.'

But the engine wouldn't start, no matter in which posi-

178

tion we placed the throttle. 'The lid's got to come off,' I said. 'There's fuck-all else for it.'

'But, Dad!' protested Rory. 'Look at the waves! They're going over the engine.'

'Rory! There's nothing else we can do. Look. Let's see if we can time it between the waves. I'll whip the lid off, you clamp one hand over the mouth of the carburettor and apply the choke. Then I'll slap the lid on.'

I can still see the frustrated horror on his face as a big wave we hadn't expected came hurtling over the stern, over the unprotected engine and over his head. He grabbed the side of the canoe to stop him going on into the sea with the wave, and the engine filled with water through the mouth of the carburettor. We were now completely dead ducks. There was absolutely nothing we could do. We were at the mercy of the waves which were sending us further and further from the shore and the marker buoy.

It is easy to write that for nearly an hour we were tossed this way and that. But each minute was a very long one. Redmond was in another world with the agony of his seasickness. Yeannie, too, was like a marble statue, the only difference being that her lips were moving in prayer. Rory and I fought grimly with the oars to try to give us some form of counteraction against the waves. Also, I finished off the whisky.

It was Yeannie who first saw the fishing trawler. She had been bruised too much in the sitting position and had decided to stand up. She suddenly started waving a white pillow slip. Rory and I then saw the trawler, and we, too, began waving with our shirts.

Thankfully, after what seemed an eternity, the trawler turned towards us. She disappeared many, many times behind the waves before she reached us.

'What are you doing out here?' the captain bellowed. 'Going to your deaths? No one crosses this part of the waters.'

He manoeuvred alongside, the two craft thudding and crunching against each other, and a rope was thrown.

179

After much difficulty our canoe, which was longer than the trawler, was tied alongside.

'Let us get out of here, fast,' urged the captain. 'I will tow you back to calmer waters by the long bridge where you can put down anchor for the night. Then I must be off or I will miss the fish.'

It was heavenly to feel the power of the trawler's engine pushing us to safety. It was almost dark when we reached the comparative calm of the water, some 100 metres from the bridge, and I shuddered to think what we would now be doing right out there in the twilight, and then the darkness.

I offered the captain money but he said he preferred petrol, and he siphoned off a good five gallons before he departed. We put down anchor and it bit instantly and held.

'Dad,' said Rory, with complete resolve in his voice, 'that's it. I am not going out again in this boat. I'd rather borrow the money and fly to England. I'd be broke afterwards, but at least I'd be alive.'

'Yes, Gerald,' said Yeannie. 'You've had your try – be satisfied that you've built a boat. But you must have a proper engine, Gerald. You know that. Like Rory, I will never go out in this boat again. I love you – love you very, very much. But I want to live, Gerald – even without you, though my heart would be broken – and if you want to continue with this crazy idea, then you must do it alone.'

'All right, all right, all right,' I said, despondently. 'But it's going to cost a hell of a lot of money to get home by plane.'

'But as Rory said, we will be alive.' She kissed me on the lips. 'I know how unhappy you feel. You failed at being Robinson Crusoe, you didn't find paradise on the Galapagos and this boat project has also been a failure. But we have each other. And you have three people who love you very much – even risked their lives for you – so I think you have more riches than most people. Supposing Redmond had drowned out there, or been killed by a shark – your life would be ruined – our lives would be

180

ruined – by the tragedy. For you never would be able to forget.'

'You're quite right,' I said, rubbing my hand over my eyes. 'God, I feel tired. I think I'll make some coffee.' I returned her kiss and turned to Rory. 'Take the plugs out, pour petrol into the carburettor and flush the engine through by pulling the starter cord.' I told Redmond to get off the wet floor and go to bed and I would take him some coffee. 'Make sure you keep yourself warm,' I added. 'You may have a bit of shock in you and not realise it.'

Yeannie lit two candles and began picking things up from where they had tumbled into the water that had come over the side and through the clinker planking.

'How's the coffee plant?' I asked her.

'Fine,' she said. 'Look, I covered it with a plastic bag so that the salt water wouldn't get to it.'

I felt very disconsolate as I wiped the cups and put in the coffee, powdered milk and sugar, making sure that Redmond's cup had more milk and sugar than coffee. I knew the boat was sound, and virtually unsinkable. If only we'd had a good, powerful engine – or even a sail. But the mast, being mangrove, had gone straight to the bottom like a piece of iron. If only we had put everything below decks . . . If only we had left by the proper channel . . . If only Redmond hadn't tried to sleep on the deck . . . Ifs, ifs, ifs. If only we'd had more time – time to finish the boat properly. Time to have made a test run, not put straight to sea.

Rory's sudden yell stopped further commiseration. 'Dad! Dad! The engine's on fire!'

I went outside, cursing. Flames were all over the engine. I knew what Rory had done – or rather had not done: insulate the HT leads. The spark, when he pulled the starter cord, had ignited the petrol shooting out of the plug holes with the compression. 'Well, put the pissing thing out,' I told him, and threw him a soaking wet sheet. 'Put that over it and suffocate it – then come on in – coffee's ready.'

We decided that we'd both had enough of Yamaha 15

181

engines for one day, and, after coffee, went to bed. Rory elected to sleep fully clothed on a pile of unused planking under the stars, rather than under the deck. I lay awake with my thoughts for a long time, and I knew that Yeannie was a long time awake with hers.

Something woke me unnaturally at first light, and I gave a chuckle when I realised what it was. The Canadian accent, even in song, was unmistakable:

'Rule, Britannia,
Britannia, rule the waves!
Britons never, never, never shall be slaves!'

I went outside and there was Jerry, leaning on the rail of the bridge by the side of the jeep that was taking him to the airport.

'The engine's fucked,' I called to him.

He waved in acknowledgement. 'My driver will organise a tow when he gets back from the airport. Don't forget to send me a copy of your book. Call it "Another Failure"!' He laughed quite heartily. 'Gotta go. Good luck!'

I was determined I wasn't going to suffer any further humiliation by being towed back past all those staring eyes in Tumaco. After breakfast, I took the spark plugs and put them on a piece of tin plate on the stove. Then I insulated the HT leads with cloth and gave the engine a good flush through with petrol. Finally, I put in the hot plugs. Rory applied the choke and held the throttle open to the correct place while I pulled the starter cord. The engine fired and ran on the third pull, just as one of Plan's concrete fishing boats came out from under the bridge.

I told the two men on board that we were OK and that we would go in under our own steam. They chugged alongside to make sure everything was all right. People stood on rooftops and on the shore between houses and stores to watch us go by, on to Plan's wharf. Rory, Redmond and Yeannie stood for'ard near the bow, assuming an air of feigned imperviousness, ignoring the

182

stares and arms pointing at us. I drew in next to another trawler and made fast.

As I stopped the engine, Redmond walked back to me. 'I wouldn't mind having another go at it, Dad,' he said.

'Neither would I,' I replied, 'but those other two are adamant that they're not going out again.'

'Well why don't just the two of us go?'

'Are you serious? You'd really go out there again?'

'Yes,' he said. 'I wasn't at all frightened. Not even when I went overboard. This boat is bloody good, and I doubt if we'd ever be in a rougher sea than that.'

Admiration for him welled inside me. 'Hey, you two!' I called. 'Redmond wants to have another try!'

'Get stuffed,' said Rory.

'Gerald, don't be so stupid!' exclaimed Yeannie, with great alarm.

But the decision not to venture out again was not with me and Redmond. News travelled fast in Tumaco; the port captain's PA came aboard, all condolences. 'I must ask you for your papers,' he said. 'I cannot let you go out there again unless you have a sail and a better engine.'

Before I sadly handed him the registration document and the very colourful and beautiful 'Zarpe' – international certificate – I studied the latter as though to memorise it. It had the Colombian crest in yellow on a blue background. Beneath the words of authorisation, it said 'The Islander'. Captain: Gerald Kingsland. Engineer: Rory Kingsland. Crew: Redmond Kingsland, Yeannie Ackermann. I had been a sea captain for a day – and I'd made a complete balls of it.

'If you will come to my office as soon as possible,' the PA continued, with politeness and regret, 'I will refund you all your money.'

'Thank you very much,' I said, quietly. 'That is very decent of you.'

While we were waiting for the tide to be high enough to pass under the small bridge, many people came on board to have a look round. One of them was an old negro fisherman.

'You are very lucky to be alive,' he said. 'You should never have gone that way. Two wrecks lie on the bottom out there.'

All the Benitezes, except for Mercedes, who had gone to Spain to visit her daughter, came down the beach as we pulled in, crestfallen and exhausted. They were full of apologies.

'I am very sorry,' said Alex. 'But you did want to leave as soon as possible and there was no alternative but to go that route.'

'I know,' I said.

'What will you do now?' asked Hugo.

'Get to Bogota' as soon as possible and contact the British Embassy.'

'I will organise a sale of the boat and engine and anything else you want to sell to pay for your air fares,' said Alex.

And he did. We got 30,000 pesos for the engine, 12,000 for the boat and 10,000 for the shotgun. Two days later we were in Colombia's capital where we booked into the cheapest hotel that would accept Redmond's Visa-card.

While we waited for money to come from England, via the Foreign Office and embassy, we found that the cheapest flights were through Miami. Then came a crunch. The American Embassy refused point-blank to grant Yeannie a transit visa. And the British Consul told me that he very much doubted if she would be allowed into England without a return ticket. It was then that I cursed the stupidity and pettiness of bureaucracy. 'What do you think she is going to do? Blow up the country?' I stormed, but to no avail.

There was nothing else for it – she would have to return to Chile. Sadly, I bought her ticket and gave her 100 US dollars. 'I'll do all I can to get you to England,' I promised her. She was crying and clutching her beloved coffee plant as we kissed goodbye, and there was a large lump in my throat.

Epilogue

In the middle distance of the broad, fertile valley's high, sweeping splendour stood the *alamos* – the Spanish name for poplars.

'Our house is just behind those trees,' Yeannie told me. 'You see that big, tall column of rock? That is petrified. And behind those hills live the Indians.'

We were standing close together on the very ancient and hoof-marked, hand-pulled ferry barge to cross Chile's longest river, near to where it started high in the Andes.

We got back into her cousin's Land-rover and drove along a dusty trail. 'How big is your little farm?' I asked, in wonderment.

'About 700 acres,' she replied to my astonishment. 'Then there is the mountain range for summer grazing, and it joins Argentina. And it's all ours!'

I saw that the sparkling, clear water of the fast-flowing Bio Bio river ran within fifty metres of the large ranch house. 'Wait until you see the size of the salmon and trout!' she said, as she unlocked the front door.

As she proudly showed me over the house, I counted seven bedrooms, and the dining-room was forty feet long.

'My goodness,' I exclaimed. 'It's beautiful. I feel that at last I have arrived home.'

'You never thought I was this rich when you met me in Quito, did you?'

'No,' I said. 'It's like a dream. Like a fairy tale with the difference that it's a princess, not a prince who is the charmer.'

She laughed, happily. 'I think Rory and Redmond would have more respect for me if they could see me now, and not as the little gold-digger that they always thought I was.'

'But why did you never say anything about this?'

She kissed me. 'Because I wanted to be sure of you,' she said, simply. 'We have a few cattle with which to start a herd – my father had to sell most of them to pay my mother a lump sum when she divorced him. There are a few sheep, too, four riding horses and 120 goats. Tomorrow, we will go riding. I will take the mare and you can have the grey horse. Like you, he is a little old!' She threw her arms around me, laughing, and her eyes sparkling. 'Here come our two ranch hands, Guillermo and Pascual – I will introduce you as the new boss.'

The two men came riding up on their cow ponies, leather lassoes coiled by the side of their sheepswool saddles. On their legs were goatskin chaps, on their heads, sombreros. They dismounted and tied their ponies to the hitching rail. It was like a scene from a Western.

They were obviously very pleased to see *la señorita* Yeannie. It was five years since they had seen her. They gave me brief handshakes. Their attention was solely for Yeannie.

After they had gone to the bunkhouse, Yeannie said: 'You must always show them that you are the boss – never their equal, or they will have no respect for you. It is the way of life here. I told them to have the horses ready tomorrow morning. When we have finished riding, we leave the horses here for them to see to.'

That night we ate *chivo asado* (goat roasted on a spit). As we sat sipping excellent Chilean wine afterwards, I commented with some sadness: 'I wish we had our coffee plant, don't you?'

'Oh, yes,' she said. 'I cried when customs took it away from me. It seemed to signify the end of everything.'

'But it wasn't the end,' I said, softly. 'We're together again despite everything and the problems with visas.'

She kissed me. 'Let's go to bed,' she said.

There was an instant rapport between the grey and me next morning. He had no name, so I gave him one: Herbert. Yeannie immediately showed off that she was an

186

expert horsewoman, prancing the mare backwards and forwards.

'We ride *huaso* style,' she shouted, her green eyes shining with excitement. 'One hand on the reins, the other on hips. Like this! Let's go!' And off she went at a gallop.

'Did you understand all that, Herbert?' The grey put back one ear. 'Come on! Let's go!' Herbert decided that a slow walk was quite sufficient. Yeannie came galloping back, laughing. 'I don't think he understands English,' she said, and gave Herbert a resounding thwack on his rump with the end of her reins. Herbert went into a canter. 'You must always ride by my side,' said Yeannie, 'never behind. A man who rides behind a woman is not respected.'

We slowed to a walk and left the main trail to climb up high. 'Herbert is very sure-footed,' she said, 'so don't worry how steep it is.'

At the top of a very high hill we stopped so that I could admire the view.

'Do you think you have found your paradise?' she asked.

'I am sure of it.'

'You will be happy here?'

'Oh, Yeannie, how can you ask such a thing? You know I will. It's what I've always dreamed of.'

'Good. No more stupid adventures for you. I think when we are married I would like a little girl with your nose and eyes.'

'Do you think I was crazy in Tumaco to want to sail to England in that canoe?' I asked her.

'Crazy?' she echoed, laughing. 'You were positively demented! I will always remember that word.'

Los Esquistos
Lonquimay
Chile

Acknowledgements and thanks

There are many people I would like to thank for assisting me on this adventure. Foremost should be Jerry Vink, director of Plan de Padrinos, Tumaco, Colombia, for his invaluable assistance when I needed it most. Next, Alex Benitez, his father and mother, Hugo and Mercedes, and his wife, Sonia, who proved to be the nicest of neighbours.

Also in Tumaco, Señora de Lopez, proprietress of the Hotel Don Pepe; the captain of the port, Capitán Daniel Gutierrez; his very helpful and likable Personal Assistant whose name, I'm afraid, I have no record of; the Major of Marines; and Panchano, the naval architect. Then, of course, in the Colombian jungle, Maximino, Onofre and all the other villagers who came to our aid.

On the Galapagos Islands: Oscar and Negra Tricallotis.

On the M/v *Buccaneer*: the proprietors, Gordontours of Guayaquil; the purser, the Hon. Claiborne Mitchell; and Clarice Strang, a nature guide.

In Quito: Lucho and Ana Fiallos.

In the Andean village of Pususquere: Mercedes Guerrero, 'Tia Maria', Señora Amparo, 'Megaphone' and, of necessity, Lola Guerrero, for without her we would never have gone to Colombia.

In England: the Nosworthys of Rowden Paddocks, Bromyard, Herefordshire; Whitby & Co of Cumberland, for the beautiful knives they donated; and the late Jim Bouston, of Bromyard, who sadly died just before my return to England – a true friend who lent me his invaluable clasp knife which I will always remember him by.

I must also thank Arthur for the use of his canoe.

My sincere gratitude to all of you. I will never forget you. Nor will I forget the five nuns who blessed our boat. As Yeannie always maintains, it was probably their blessing which saved us from drowning. Though, of course, God did have the unsinkable trunk of a giant ceibo tree to help him!

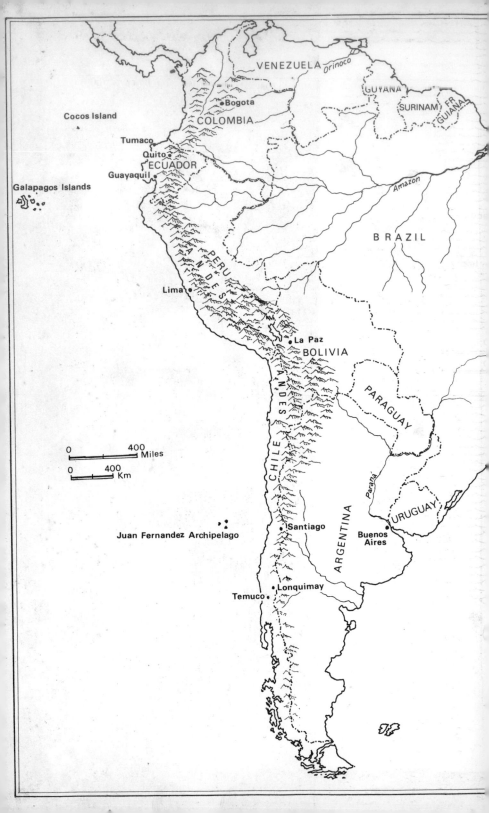